Spirituality:
Transformation
Within and Without

Swami Rama

The Himalayan Institute Press
Honesdale, Pennsylvania

The Himalayan Institute Press
RR 1, Box 405
Honesdale, PA 18431

Cover design by Robert Aulicino

The paper used in this publication meets the minimum
requirements of the American National Standard for
Information Sciences—Permanence of Paper for Printed
Library Materials, ANSI Z39.48-1984.

ISBN 0-89389-150-9

CONTENTS

FOREWORD

THIRTY-THREE YEARS AGO Swami Rama conceived this book on the banks of the holy Ganges, in the city of Allahabad, in India. In those days Swamiji lived in a beautiful place now known as Shiva Kuti, situated on the outskirts of the city, and while enjoying solitude there, he participated in the *kumbha mela*—the grandest spiritual festival in India. In the winter of 1964, at the invitation of Vishva Hindu Parishad, Swamiji delivered a series of lectures on religion and spirituality at the kumbha mela which awakened tens of thousands of hearts from religious and intellectual slumber. Those who heard him felt as if their heads were on fire when Swamiji blasted hypocrisy, sectarianism, blind faith, the caste system, and the oppression of women. Those who believed firmly in temples and priestly ritualistic ceremonies were amazed to hear that spirituality cannot be confined within the walls of temples, mosques, and churches. And as they continued listening they realized that spirituality can be practiced without dependence on others, that they can experience God in their day-to-day lives.

Those who held the preconceived notion that a swami is a Hindu religious leader, who must therefore advocate Hinduism, were distressed to hear that Swamiji did not have a special preference for any religion. Swamiji drew a clear distinction between Hinduism and *sanatana dharma* ("the eternal teaching"), as outlined in the Vedas. He reminded the crowd that the Vedas do not belong to Hindus or Indians exclusively, but are a treasure-house of the theories and practices pertaining to the eternal truth that belongs to all humanity.

A number of leaders of Hinduism and their followers were outraged when they heard Swamiji claiming that other religions are as good as Hinduism, and that belonging to a particular religion is one thing, while practicing the spiritual principles and the higher values of life propounded in that religion is something else. Those following a Hindu religious leader blindly, Swamiji said, are like Hindu sheep, and those who blindly follow Christianity are like Christian sheep—but, ultimately, they are all sheep. Those who embrace the teachings of the Bhagavad Gita or the Bible in their daily lives, however, are transformed from sheep to human, and they alone are true Hindus and Christians. Such sincere and honest practitioners will one day be blessed with the knowledge of eternal truth, Swamiji continued, saying that thereafter their consciousness will expand beyond the territories of any religion.

As the kumbha mela is visited mainly by devout Hindu pilgrims, some in the audience were exhilarated, and others were upset. Swamiji became the center of controversy, and the controversy attracted even larger crowds. And as the crowds grew, Swamiji began to add more fuel to the fire. He had a unique style. He always started his lectures in a very gentle, loving manner. At the climax of each presentation he turned into a raging storm blowing away misconceptions about God, heaven, hell, and dependence on priests and pandits. But soon his stormy self would subside, and he would again become a gentle saint. In this masterful way he would channel the sentiments of his listeners toward the universal teachings of the sages, and convince them that truth can be experienced not by listening to lofty discourses but by practicing spiritual techniques. Through these alone, he told them, can they gain direct experience of the truth within.

All those listening to his words were deeply affected. Those broad-minded souls open and receptive to the truth—whether highly educated and well-to-do, or illiterate and penniless—were thrilled and infused with spiritual light and warmth. But narrow-minded souls—especially Hindu priests and astrologers who lived as swamis—were angry. Several months after the kumbha mela, Swamiji remained the main topic of discussion.

Meanwhile a group of students compiled his lectures, which with Swamiji's guidance were published in Hindi in 1966 under the title *Yuga Dharma Kya* [What Is Eternal Dharma?]. Later Swamiji revised and expanded this book and published it in Hindi in the 1980s under the title *Dharma Aur Samaj Man Kranti* [Revolution in Religion and Society]. Then in 1988 Swamiji translated this book into English, and it was published by the Himalayan Institute as *A Call to Humanity: Revolutionary Thoughts on the Direction for Spiritual and Social Reform in Our Time*. The present volume, *Spirituality: Transformation Within and Without*, is a revised version of *A Call to Humanity*. It has been slightly edited, and in places new material has been added.

For me there can be no greater pleasure than presenting this book to spiritual seekers all over the world, for in these pages Swamiji opens our eyes to the truth within, and to the manifestation of that truth in the outside world. I am certain that readers will use this volume as a manual for self-transformation as well as a source of inner inspiration. I sincerely thank Linda Johnsen, who edited and put the final touches on the manuscript, and the Himalayan Institute staff, whose cooperative efforts have made its publication possible.

Pandit Rajmani Tigunait

CHAPTER ONE

THE EXISTENCE OF GOD

BELIEF IN THE EXISTENCE OF GOD shows that one is searching for truth. Truth is that which is unborn and immortal, and remains unchanged in the past, present, and future. To know it, one needs to purify one's thoughts, speech, and actions. Purification is of utmost importance because only through a purified mind can an aspirant think clearly and contemplate deeply. Once we are sincerely determined to search for the truth and fully committed to self-purification, we are certain to find the way and reach our goal. Truth itself becomes our guide and we find ourselves on the right path.

Truth is that divine force which dwells in every individual's heart. It is the all-pervading, eternal reality joining one individual to another, and linking all existence in one divine awareness. That divine force is called God. One who believes in and surrenders himself to God attains freedom here and now. He knows that he belongs to God—and God belongs to him. His awareness shifts from the world to God, and he lives a life free from insecurity and fear. He has an unshakable faith in divine protection. The scriptures constantly remind us that just as the ocean accepts a river and makes it its own, so God receives all who sincerely seek the Divine. It does not matter which path they follow or from which background they come. The only requirement is a desire to know the truth. Once that desire is awakened, all means and resources come together. Water finds its own level; likewise, a true lover of God finds God. The highest philosophy is to know that truth and God are one and the same, and the highest practice is to search for truth through one's thoughts, speech, and actions.

Belief in God and experiencing the presence of God in every moment are two different things. Before the actual direct experience of truth, a human being may believe in the existence of God, but true faith comes only after personal experience. Faith born from direct experience protects the aspirant like a mother protects her child. Initially, in the developmental process, the desire to search for God manifests in the form of curiosity. Like a child, the aspirant first wonders about truth, then asks questions and searches for answers from the outside world. He discovers that intellectual satisfaction is not sufficient, and ultimately he is inspired to know the truth directly from within. Questioning is the first step in the search for the truth.

Truth is absolute, transcendent, and unmanifest. One single, nondual reality manifests in the external world in countless names and forms. From the very beginning of our childhood we are taught to believe in the multiplicity of external objects, in the reality of names and forms. Consequently, as we grow older we fail to comprehend the existence of nondual truth. If we change our educational system and inspire our children to contemplate the truth at an early age, they will be able to recognize the truth, the source of their inner potential, much more easily than those who have gone through a learning process that emphasizes duality.

By forgetting the absolute nondual truth and believing in the existence of illusory external objects, we pollute our minds and dissipate our inner potential. If we are curious, we search for truth in the outer world, but no matter how much curiosity we have, if our inner resources are not awakened, we waste our time and energy. Spiritual practices, undertaken at an early age, have a profound and long-lasting effect.

Without exception, every human being wants peace and happiness, but out of laziness or negligence most fail to achieve the objects of their desires. The desire to know the truth and to experience it directly is certainly important, but the most important factor for an aspirant is to overcome laziness and negligence. Through continuous practice and sincere effort, an aspirant can conquer these two great enemies. Due to lack of practice, a potentially invincible human being loses the battle. Consciously or unconsciously, every human being knows the purpose of life, but being unaware of the appropriate means to pursue it, he fails to attain the goal. The first step toward the realization of the truth is to know the proper method of practice. The second step is to practice it faithfully and regularly, for a prolonged period of time. This is possible if an aspirant applies the following three golden rules:

1. Be aware of the goal and work toward it all the time.
2. Make the best use of your time.
3. Be happy in every situation in life.

An aspirant must learn how to use the objects of the world as means; he must learn not to get caught up in the charms and temptations of objects.

For a spiritually inspired couple, the marital relationship is a means for spiritual upliftment. While living in the world, if a wife and husband can become a means for each other's spiritual achievement, then they can both reach the goal quite happily and effectively. However, if each views the other as an object for sensual fulfillment, then they miss the purpose of life. Wife, husband, children, family, wealth, and the objects of the world are meant for *sadhana*, spiritual practice. But, out of ignorance, a householder's life is usually devoid of spiritual motivation. Consequently, householders become attached to relationships and the objects they own. Attachment brings unending bondage that can be overcome only by sadhana.

It is good to love others and to have a positive attitude toward worldly objects, but one must not become attached to them. By knowing the difference between love and attachment, one can change one's worldview and make the best use of objects. Through gradual purification and transformation, one can change attachment into pure love and thereby turn weakness into a source of strength. Out of ignorance, a person considers himself to be the owner of worldly objects. He gets attached to the objects and suffers as a result of loss and gain. Attachment signifies an act in which ego claims to be the owner of the object it possesses, whereas love for the object indicates the surrender of the ego to the higher force to whom all the objects of the world truly belong. Thus, attachment is the source of bondage, whereas love is the source of liberation. In the light of pure love, one attains a nondual state, but driven by attachment, one confines oneself within the walls of ego.

There are two kinds of beliefs: those which grow through observation, and those which have direct experience as their source. The first kind takes place in early childhood when the heart is pure. We believe in whatever we hear or see. At this stage, when we hear a word, its corresponding meaning flashes in our mind. The mind considers the word and its meaning to be real. Along with the relationship between the word and its meaning, a visual image is imprinted in the mindfield. In childhood the mind is like blank paper on which anything can be written. Input at this stage creates a permanent impression, and the child believes in the reality of that object. With purity and openness, he believes all he hears. As a child grows, his trusting nature disappears. From one standpoint, childhood can be considered a stage of blind faith, because the child does not feel the necessity to verify the validity of the things he trusts. His belief is not illumined either with the light of direct experience, or of logic and reasoning.

The other kind of belief originates from the direct experience of truth. Belief based on direct experience is self-evident, requiring no proof for its validity. As a child grows, the intellectual part of his personality evolves, and as a result, he seeks intellectual verification of his earlier beliefs. If satisfied intellectually, he maintains his beliefs, otherwise he discards them completely. However, his intellectual conviction can stand firm only if it is supported by direct experience. Both blind belief and intellectual conviction are overshadowed by direct experience.

The kind of company we keep and the kind of environment in which we live have an indelible impact on our growth. A mind clouded by nonconstructive beliefs during early childhood can become a great barrier in later stages of life. However, if at that tender age a child has the privilege of living with evolved souls, he naturally becomes influenced by their great qualities. He absorbs their higher qualities and believes in higher virtues. The seeds of belief in higher truths sprout, grow, and ultimately bloom. The purity of his heart and innocence is retained. One day, such a fortunate one experiences the truth directly since his faith is pure and firm.

Once childhood is gone and the intellect has taken over, we must verify our beliefs. A belief established on the solid foundation of truth is a source of strength. A belief based on the direct experience of the truth, not contradicted by logic and reasoning, is known as *shraddha* or faith. Such faith is established over an extended period of time. Repeated experiences add to the maturity of the faith. Direct experience of the truth removes all doubts and leads an aspirant to a decisive understanding. Knowledge becomes firm; he does not feel it necessary to seek verification from others. He knows that he knows; such is his faith. On the basis of that faith, he starts his quest and reaches his goal. Ordinarily people do not have such faith; rather they live with mere beliefs. Faith in God leads one to God; mere belief in God may lead to a series of disappointments.

In every part of the world, stories told about the lives of the saints and sages are replete with incidents that are beyond ordinary comprehension. No matter how much one intellectualizes or how doubtful one remains, at a certain point in life, one has to accept the existence of the divine force which functions behind all other forces of nature.

Even our thinking processes receive their power from that infinite divine force. Being omnipresent, the divine force

from each other, like the pot having both clay and potter as causes. However, in the case of the manifestation of the world, there is only one cause, that is God. As supreme consciousness, God is the efficient cause of the universe. At the same time, without relying on any material cause, God spontaneously lets the universe manifest through his unrestricted power of will. Philosophically speaking, the power of will can be construed as the material cause of the universe, but since the power of will is intrinsic to God, God alone becomes the material cause as well. According to the sages, through his power of will, God alone shines in numerous forms and names. Viewed from the standpoint of the manifest world, one experiences constant change, transformation, death, and decay, but viewed from the absolute reality, there is no change, transformation, death, or decay at all.

The all-pervading, eternal, pure consciousness is conscious of its nondual existence, as well as being conscious of the entire diversified, manifest world. Without going through any change or transformation, consciousness witnesses the entire drama played by its descending and ascending forces. That uninvolved, pure witness is God. Those who experience God within become pure mirrors to reflect God to novice seekers. In their hearts God resides, and in their presence the light of God emanates. An aspirant's heart is purified and his mind is turned inward when he hears about the glory of God from such an enlightened sage. In the company of a sage spontaneous faith arises, which cannot be shaken by the forces of logic or reasoning. In fact, with the awakening of such faith, the intellect surrenders to the virtues of the heart and humbly uses the logic and reasoning to support and substantiate the truth.

Once an aspirant is inspired and doubts are removed, he is fully prepared to undertake spiritual practices. Such an aspirant is called an awakened one. An awakened student makes efforts to seek the company of sages. He prostrates at their feet and humbly requests a practice. Moved by his humility and purity of heart, the compassionate sage instructs the student in the right method of practice. Without exception, such a blessed student reaches the goal.

Practice is divided into three main stages:

Initial: At this stage, the student thinks he is practicing, but actually he is preparing himself for practice. His so-called practice consists of learning the necessary techniques and collecting the resources to begin the quest and stay on the path.

Intermediate: At this stage, a student is fully equipped with all the resources he needs to practice. His time and energy are not involved in learning methods, rather he spends his time in actual practice.

Final: At this stage, a student experiences the truth. He may have only a momentary glimpse, but at least it is a direct experience, which helps him understand the greatness of his goal. Now sadhana consists of trying to maintain that state. As his practice matures, he becomes an adept; then he no longer needs to keep trying, for the experience of nondual reality is maintained effortlessly and spontaneously.

Out of thousands of people interested in spirituality, only a few aspirants devote time to the study of spiritual texts. Most of those who study are satisfied with the study itself; they do not actually practice what they've learned. As a result, they become confused by the apparently contradictory teachings of the books. According to some scriptures, reality is nondual; according to others, God and soul are two different principles. According to one, God is real and the universe is unreal, whereas according to others, both God and the universe are equally real. For nonpracticing readers, it is difficult to understand which philosophy is right and which is wrong. For a practitioner, however, all of those statements are equally valid experiences at different stages along the path. Therefore he uses these theories as guidelines for contemplation. A practitioner never relies on philosophical thinking alone. His spiritual life consists of contemplation and meditation. For him, philosophical debates are a waste of time.

Yogis know that before reaching the realization of nondual reality, an aspirant passes through multileveled experiences of manifest and unmanifest reality. The experiences belonging to manifest reality support the duality of the truth, and the experiences belonging to unmanifest absolute reality confirm the nondual truth. Minor differences in inner experience belong to the period of transition from manifest to unmanifest and from immanent to transcendent. Through his prolonged practice and the grace of God, when an aspirant merges in his *Ishta Devata,* the inner reality, he experiences the nondual truth. In that, he transcends the trinity of knower, the process of knowing, and the object of knowledge. He becomes one with the truth. That is the state that scriptures describe in mystic language: "The knower of the truth becomes the truth; the knower and the known are one and the same." By rising above the sense of ego, an aspirant knows that which ought to be known. He realizes his identity with pure existence, consciousness, and bliss. Upon that realization, he experiences the existence of the divine force in all his thoughts, speech, and actions.

Knowing a particle of gold, in essence we know the

entire lump of gold. Likewise, by knowing an individual body and mind, we can unveil the secret of the universe. That which lies in the universe lies in the body, and vice versa. Upon knowing the truth within, one realizes the truth which stands behind the existence of the universe. If we do not accept the existence of God, then how can we explain many of the unknown and indescribable phenomena of the universe? We cannot postpone the issue under discussion by saying, "Well, there must be some force." That force scientists consider indescribable is known to the yogis as God. If we believe in our existence, then how can we deny the collective existence of others, or of the world around us? If there is no way to deny our individual and collective existence, how can we deny the existence of that which is the source of it all? In denying the existence of God, we deny the existence of anything at all. Actually, our belief or disbelief does not affect the self-existent truth. Human beings are caught in the net of their own confusion, which can be removed through direct experience of the truth.

A human being thinks according to his nature, and his way of thinking helps him come to a conclusion. On the basis of this conclusion, he decides to act, and in accordance with his action, he obtains a result. So before he actually performs an action, there is a long and interconnected series of inner events including desire, thought, and decision. Desire is at the root of everything. In order to draw proper conclusions and perform the action appropriately, one needs to purify one's desires. Without purifying one's desires, one will not be able to organize the various aspects of life. Purification of desire requires the purification of the mind, intellect, and ego. These three are called *antahkarana*, the inner instrument. Purification of the inner instrument helps one employ his resources rightly. A person with a purified mind, intellect, and ego purifies his desires and performs his actions while keeping the highest goal of life as his main focus. Without inner purification, a human being fails to envision the true purpose of life.

God alone is the source of a human being's inner strength; without that strength, one cannot even move. That inner strength is sometimes called willpower or self-confidence. Even atheists and nonbelievers rely on their inner strength. An atheist considers willpower to be instinctive and disregards its connection with the Divine, whereas a theist considers it to be divine and makes the best use of it. The divine force does not discriminate, and therefore sends forth inspiration equally to atheists and theists alike. Whether we believe in or disregard the existence of God, we live with that force, and it is only through that force that the journey of life continues.

Those who know that their willpower, confidence, inner strength, and intellect receive their inspiration from the very fountainhead of the divine force become humble, gentle, loving, and considerate to all. They know that nothing belongs to them; all powers belong to God. On the other hand, those who do not see the source, but take their strength, courage, and intellectual understanding for granted become egotistical and inconsiderate of others. Thus, belief or disbelief, respect or disrespect, do not make any difference to the divine force itself; it is the individual who is benefited by his own faith in the Divine.

Until our whole being is illuminated with the light of truth, there is no hope of attaining freedom from pain and misery. Illumination is not in our hands— purification is our part of the process. Faith in God is the way to purify our mind and heart. Once purification is accomplished, we experience the illumination of the Divine which already exists in our heart. Faith in God does not mean believing that God lives in heaven, way up in the sky. God, who lives in your heart and in the hearts of others, and who manifests in the form of the universe, can help us cultivate higher human virtues. Only from such a God can we achieve freedom from all pain and misery.

It seems that there is a subtle and invisible force that guides the destiny of not only human beings but the whole of creation. Whenever it is needed, this benevolent force takes over and restores law and order in society, community, and nation. As the history of ancient India reminds us, when the priests began exploiting the Vedic ceremonies, and when the slaughter of animals became part of the rituals, Buddha was born. He reformed society, altered religious practices, and brought relief to the oppressed members of society. However, with the passage of time, people distorted his teachings. Buddhism, which discarded sensual indulgence and drinking, became a victim of wine and sensuality. When the monks started taking advantage of the innocence of the people, and became a burden to society, then the divine force sent a brilliant scholar, yogi, and philosopher known as Shankaracharya.

Shankaracharya reestablished the Vedic teachings, reformed Indian society, and replaced blind dogmas and superstitions with the profound teachings of the Upanishads. Placing greater emphasis on knowledge, he discouraged ritualism. Through his impressive personality and his spiritual insight, he restructured religious values, set forth a nondualistic system of thought, and helped people understand the importance of spiritual knowledge. Within a century, how-

ever, his followers became obsessed with criticizing and re-
futing other paths in order to emphasize the importance of
their own. The path of knowledge as set forth by
Shankaracharya was imbued with love, devotion, and selfless
service; but under his followers, it degenerated into a mere
intellectual exercise. Consequently, the subtle divine force
chose another saint, Ramanuja, to refute the excessive intellectualism of Vedanta. When Ramanuja appeared, there
arose a wave of love and devotion which swept all over India
from south to north and west to east.

With the passage of time, these interconnected paths of
knowledge and love again fell victim to philosophical quib-
bling, losing their main foundation—spiritual practice.
Then, Madhusudhana Saraswati was born, a saint in whom
one finds a perfect balance of love, devotion, and selfless
service. In his commentary on the Bhagavad Gita,
Madhusudhana Saraswati clarifies the philosophical and spiritual statements of dualistic and nondualistic Vedanta. He
explains how the worship of a personal God is the initial step
toward experiencing the absolute nondual state of God.
From a spiritual standpoint, he offers a unique blend of love,
knowledge, and selfless action. Later, in the eighteenth century, when *dharma* again declined, Swami Dayananda appeared to reiterate this message.

Examples of divine intervention can be observed in every
area of community life. Just as an individual goes through
different stages as he grows from childhood to youth, and
from youth to old age, a society, nation, and humanity move
from one stage to another.

The forces of nature follow the will of the Divine. Nature
is not independent. Those who consider this manifest
cosmos to be the primordial truth do not recognize the

existence of the great divine force behind it. While it is true that under the direction of nature, this universe goes through the process of creation and annihilation, knowers of the truth never consider unconscious nature to be the cause or final refuge of the universe. The power of the will of the supreme divine force manifests in the form of nature. The beauty of the Divine is reflected in the mirror of nature. Those who have eyes can see divine beauty reflected in the various aspects of nature. Through its endless mountain ranges, waves of the ocean, twinkling stars, vast sky, deserts and forests, nature expresses the beauty of the Divine. How pitiful it is to deny the existence of God!

Can the unconscious force of matter determine the destiny of the conscious life-stream? Does life beget life accidentally or through the chemical reaction of material elements? Is there any force known to scientists which determines the size, characteristics, and capacity of small entities like sperm? In a drop of seminal fluid there are millions of sperm, all containing the complete seed of an enormous force of life. One microcosmic, living entity called sperm combines with an egg and thereafter grows into a child. Can chemistry or anatomy explain the physical structure of a woman—why and how a child grows and is so carefully protected in the mother's womb? From where do the sperm and egg get the power to produce a baby similar to the parents? Is it just because of the genes which supposedly carry all the characteristics of the mother and father? From where do the genes, being so small, get such power? Is it just a chemically induced phenomenon that at the moment a baby is born, the mother's breasts are filled with milk?

The human body seems to be an abode of wonders. What can be more mysterious than our own body and mind?

Certainly, there is a force that is divine, self-conscious, and self-guided. By knowing and taking refuge in that divine force, we attain eternal bliss. From birth to death, human beings go through innumerable experiences, pleasant and unpleasant. But still they never lose the hope that one day they will achieve what ought to be achieved. Our inner longing never stops because we are searching not for a limited, mortal, or temporary happiness, but for the eternal, immortal bliss which is our inner self.

One cannot refute the existence of God by intellectual analysis or logical deduction. Hundreds of thousands of people in the past have directly experienced God. They cannot all be liars; all of their experiences cannot be imaginary. How confused human beings are—they doubt the sincerity of the beloved sons and devotees of God. How sad it is that human beings doubt the honesty and simplicity of sages who have truth as their eternal friend.

Those who do not believe in the existence of God may strive hard to achieve peace and happiness, but their attempts will be in vain. They know that by no means can material objects provide complete satisfaction. Without shifting one's focus from the external to the inner life, desires grow inordinately, and there is no way to satisfy them. Believing in God means transforming one's attitudes, which comes with purification and surrender to the divine force within.

A person who does not know God as such, but who practices truthfulness, nonviolence, self-discipline, and non-possessiveness in his thoughts, speech, and actions, is a genuine theist. On the other hand, those who do not respect and practice higher human virtues, though they worship God, are virtually atheists. One attains God through one's virtuous deeds and then worships God by maintaining God-awareness. On the other hand, by indulging in nonvirtuous deeds, a worshiper of God is actually avoiding the direct experience of God and lives a life of hypocrisy.

It is useless to deny or argue the existence of God. Every human being accepts God in one way or another, in one form or another. The highest good lies in believing in and finding God. Humans are considered to be the best of all species because they can cultivate divine qualities and can strive to become one with the Divine. However, a human being will retard his growth by not believing in God. A person who believes this physical world is the sole reality confines the purpose of his life to his experience of sense pleasures and the accumulation of worldly objects. He works hard to collect objects and is afraid of losing them. Even when he recognizes the insignificance of worldly objects, still he doesn't know what else to look for. Deep down in his heart, even the most successful materialistic person is insecure, dissatisfied, and fearful. Those who believe in God enjoy the objects of the world with better understanding than atheists. They know that these objects are given to them by the Divine and are meant to be employed as tools to experience the Divine. Such a person enjoys these objects with full awareness that one day he will leave them behind and merge into the Divine. On the other hand, a materialist accumulates stress and tension as he accumulates material objects, and lives a life full of insecurity and fear.

We cannot escape from our inherent longings, yet we cannot postpone our utmost need. In addition to our primitive urges for food, sex, sleep, and self-preservation, there is a higher urge to merge with God. We cannot be at peace unless that inherent divine urge is fulfilled. We all want to experience that all-pervading, omnipresent God from which the entire universe, as well as each individual, evolves. The direct experience of the truth that each of us originates from God, and ultimately ends in God, makes us secure, happy, and strong. Fearlessness comes from knowing that God is with us, and we are with God.

Today, people all over the world are busy collecting material objects. All their energy is focused on the external world. Collecting objects is destructive to mankind. Means and resources can throw one into the blind darkness of worry and regret if one does not have a constructive purpose in life. This constructive purpose can be imparted by a change in the system of education. Today millions of educated men and women are suffering from a lack of purpose. Lacking also in self-confidence, young girls and boys have become victims of dissatisfaction and frustration. Along with worldly education, we must provide some spiritual education. Spirituality must not be influenced by a particular religion, sect, or cult. As a part of our educational training, we must define spirituality in its most precise and universal terms. Spirituality means that which helps us discipline our thoughts, speech, and actions, which leads us toward the center of consciousness, and thereby unfolds our inner potentials. Education based on such spiritual guidelines will help humanity become self-reliant, confident, and active in the external world. At the same time, it will enable humanity to broaden its worldview, and to turn inward to search for the perennial truth. Only a spiritually-based education can bring a harmonious balance to our external and internal lives.

Knowledge of the theories that prove the existence of God is not as important as learning to discipline oneself so that God can be experienced directly. Children should be taught how to sit quietly and make their minds one-pointed. Through their calm and one-pointed minds, children can obtain a glimpse of true peace and happiness. We need not force them to believe there is a God. However, we should provide them with the opportunity to unfold their inner potentials, gain confidence, and become inspired to search for God, according to their own inner tendencies and backgrounds. Believers of all faiths, clinging to external rituals, impose their ideals on their children, forcing them to participate in their time-honored customs. The children are asked to love and worship pictures of Christ, Krishna, or other gods and goddesses, and sometimes even community or religious leaders. This does not help children to become independent. Today, children need to cultivate divine virtues within themselves; they need to look within, find within, and attain freedom.

CHAPTER TWO

RELIGION AND THE PERENNIAL TRUTH

THE WORDS *RELIGION* AND *DHARMA* denote two entirely different concepts and perspectives. Religion is composed of rituals, customs, and dogmas surviving on the basis of fear and blind faith. Dharma—a word, unfortunately, with no English equivalent—encapsulates those great laws and disciplines which uphold, sustain, and ultimately lead humanity to the sublime heights of worldly and spiritual glory. Established in the name of God, a religion is an institution that requires a growing number of adherents for its expansion and future existence. A religion discriminates against human beings who do not belong to it and condemns their way of living and being, whereas the perennial truth of dharma is eternal, needing no followers for its propagation. Without discriminating against anyone, it leads a human being beyond the realms of man-made, institutionalized dictums. Instead of creating fear of God, it helps us find God in our own hearts, not in an anthropomorphic form, but as the absolute and universal One in whom all beings and all things reside in perfect harmony.

Dharma shines in the form of truthfulness, nonviolence, love, compassion, forbearance, forgiveness, and sharing. A real follower of dharma includes all and excludes none. Instead of following commandments under the pressure of fear or guilt, the aspirant commits himself to discipline and self-transformation. He welcomes eternal dharma, the dharma that has as its architect none other than the divine force, the ultimate truth. The followers of dharma welcome and incorporate only those rules and laws in life that do not interfere with the growth of others, and at the same time are helpful in enhancing their creativity and helping them fulfill their purpose in life. In the history of civilization, never did a prophet or an incarnation of God introduce a "new" dharma. The sages served as channels for the perennial dharma, keeping its high ideals ever before mankind. As mentioned in the first chapter, whenever the dharma taught by the great sages seemed eclipsed, a great soul incarnated to reinspire the masses with enthusiasm for dharma.

Dharma is that which is taught by the sages, and religion is more often than not unreasoned faith. Religion is enriched by visionary mythology and theology, whereas dharma blooms in the realm of direct experience. Religion contributes to the changing phases of a culture; dharma enhances the beauty of spirituality. Religion may inspire one to build a fragile, mortal home for God; dharma helps one to recognize the immortal shrine in the heart. Religion may be an exciting field for anthropological study, producing numerous volumes of literature, but it is dharma alone that teaches one how to open the book of life and how to make the best use of all that lies therein. Religion may be helpful

in regulating a few of the primitive tendencies, such as fear
or greed, but dharma alone can help us transcend our animal instincts and step to the next rung of human awareness.

All the great religions of the world have evolved out of
the inner experiences of sages. The truths realized by the
sages were passed on from generation to generation through
an unbroken lineage of seers, and at a certain point in the
history of each tradition, people collected and preserved the
highlights of the teachings in written form. Thus, the scriptures came into existence. Sacred scriptures are considered to
be revealed texts, since the knowledge presented therein is
not based on ordinary sensory perception or mere logic and
reasoning. The wisdom of the scriptures has intuitive revelation as its source and is known through a pure heart rather
than through the limited intellect.

The Vedas are the source of a great universal tradition,
but unfortunately there are very few who are familiar with
this treasure-house of wisdom. There are several other
Eastern scriptures which explain various nuances of spiritual
life, but the seeds of even these scriptures are found in the
vast body of Vedic literature. These teachings can be understood as a tree of perennial truth. The Vedas are the roots,
the rest of the scriptures are its branches, leaves and flowers,
and the fruit of this tree is the perennial truth.

Independent thinking, contemplation, and openness can
help one realize the truth. Serious aspirants should delve
into the essence of the Vedas and Upanishads. That is possible only if one purifies and sharpens one's intellect
through positive, logical thinking. One should not be easily
influenced by the opinions of others. An opinionated
thinker fails to use his power of discrimination and remains
entangled in his self-created net of confusion.

The universal Vedic tradition is like a confluence where the streams of knowledge, selfless action, and love merge into one another. These three streams touch the three distinct but interfacing aspects of human existence—the spiritual world, the external world, and the mental/emotional world. The stream of knowledge reveals the true nature of inner life. The stream of selfless action enlivens one's relationship with the external world. Finally, the stream of love brings stability to one's mental and emotional life. By following the well-balanced path of knowledge, selfless action, and love, one attains perfection here and now. Such a seeker realizes his oneness with the universal consciousness and attains the goal professed by all religions. Every human being is endowed with three intrinsic capabilities: truth, willpower or inner strength, and love. By unfolding these potentials, one attains perfection. Therefore, according to the Vedas, the path which combines knowledge, selfless action, and love helps unfold the intrinsic potentials of truth, willpower, and selfless love, and is the essence of true religion.

The Vedic tradition welcomes any religion or faith as long as it meets these essentials of human fulfillment. Unparalleled are the Vedic ideals that declare "A religion is not religion at all if it asserts its superiority over other faiths" and "Practice only that part of the discipline which helps you to grow without hurting others." Today, humanity needs to wake up and become determined to restore high ideals, human values, and divine virtues. One must devote time to the search for the origin of one's own religion, which is never other than truth itself.

In its strictest sense, the Vedic tradition is based on the eternal law of nature. In nature, each object is unique yet all objects of the world, including all living beings, are inter-

witnesses all the states of human existence and, through all experiences from birth to death, remains unchanged. That divine force is the eternal friend of the individual self. In times of need it stands with him, guiding him in his journey from the known to the unknown, from the manifest to the unmanifest. That divine force cannot be compared to any mundane object or physical force of the world. Known as *Shakti,* the divine force is the center of consciousness. In different parts of the world, people have addressed this divine force by different names. Depending on their insight, some view it as a personal God; others consider it to be universal truth. Some consider it to be apart from the universe; others consider this universe to be a manifestation of that force. A genuine aspirant walks on the path and does not stop until he attains the experience of the totality and perfection of that truth.

The potential to realize the truth is found in every human being. In some it remains dormant, while in others it awakens. The more one directs his awareness toward the divine force, the more he realizes the emptiness of objects of the world. That realization helps him withdraw his mind from the external world, and compose himself for inner exploration. Realization of the greatness of the divine force and of the evanescence of the objects of the world results in pure *vairagya,* dispassion. In the light of dispassion or nonattachment, the aspirant attains freedom from his desires, whims, ambitions, and anxieties, and consequently, free from all distractions, he undertakes his spiritual practice wholeheartedly. Nonattachment enriches the nature of his practice. Practice combined with nonattachment helps him to continue his search until he reaches the goal.

Deep within, human beings know their present level of

knowledge is incomplete. They also know that this world has very little to offer them. Once awakened, aspirants study the nature of their own desires, whims, and ambitions, and come to the conclusion that desires cannot be fulfilled by obtaining the objects of the world. No matter how many objects they possess, the desire for more continues. Thus dissatisfaction, not fulfillment, is the inevitable outcome. Realizing that desires are not fulfilled by obtaining the desired objects is the most auspicious sign of spiritual awakening. This realization inspires one to search for the truth that transcends the sphere of mundane objects. At this realization, one attains freedom from expecting anything from the external world, and at the same time one is blessed with higher hope, courage, and vigor.

As long as a human being is confined to his ego, he fails to comprehend the higher existence of the truth. With the purification of his *samskaras,* inner tendencies, an aspirant transcends his egoism and realizes the limited value of worldly objects. The moment a person loses his interest in this mirage-like world, divine awareness dawns in his heart. As long as he remains a victim of his insatiable desires, he can neither have faith in the absolute reality, nor can he aspire to experience it.

An aspirant must control the dissipation of his mind. Conquest over the senses and the mind helps him attain freedom from the charms and temptations of the world. Free from worldly distractions, there is nothing in his mind but the longing to know God. Once such a one-pointed longing is born, he is absorbed in contemplating and meditating on God. Through his constant contemplation and meditation, he begins having glimpses of the truth which strengthen his faith. Growing internally, that one-pointed faith becomes the source of inner strength, enabling the aspirant to move along the path until perfection is achieved.

The desire to find and know the truth is a great virtue in itself. As a result of the virtuous deeds of the past, people are inspired to search for the truth. How genuinely and forcefully they search depends on how much they have purified and sharpened their intellect. As they think, contemplate, and meditate, the truth unfolds, direct experience is received, and faith is strengthened. Through the gradual unfoldment of the truth, the aspirant's confusion is removed, and he no longer mistakes blind beliefs for real faith.

The spiritual journey accelerates when the seeker realizes the transitory nature of worldly objects. He notices how limited objects and their experiences are, and gradually loses interest in sense enjoyment. His energy naturally turns inward, and he becomes determined to unveil the secret of his inner life. He resolves to transcend his worldliness and find the unlimited infinite reality. As long as an aspirant has not realized the smallness of worldly objects and the greatness of the divine force, his belief in God is weak and almost fruitless. Before this twofold realization, a human being thinks he believes in God, but in fact his belief is a mere pretense. That is why, in his day-to-day life, when he is affected by successes and failures, he begs the world for help. Fear and weakness indicate that he believes more in the world than in God. A person with faith in God cannot compromise his peace of mind with concern over worldly loss and gain. For him, every circumstance and event in life contains only the good, never the bad, because his life is guided by God.

A believer knows that God's grace flows equally to all. In the kingdom of God, there is no discrimination or sense of inequity. Since God is an embodiment of love, compassion, and auspiciousness, God never wants just a few people to be happy and the rest unhappy. Being identical to truth, his glory sheds grace uniformly without any discrimination. The sun, moon, and stars shine for all; nature dispenses his beauty and gifts for all. In the same manner, God dispenses his grace in the form of love, knowledge, and compassion equally to all living beings.

Out of ignorance a feeling of "I-am-ness" is born, forcing consciousness to feel limited, distinct, and different from the absolute truth. Because of ego, one excludes oneself from the universal self, and as a result, considers oneself separate from the omniscient, almighty God, the truth. Ignorance is the main cause of all miseries in life. Out of ignorance, one becomes attached to certain objects of the world and forgets that all objects belong to God. Out of ignorance, one begins differentiating between objects in terms of good or bad, big or small, and inferior or superior. Once that process begins, and the net of attachment and aversion is created, one finds oneself completely entangled.

"At the beginning of creation, Prajapati, the Lord of Life, alone existed. Out of his sheer will, he manifested in infinite forms." This Upanishadic assertion is a spiritual guideline for seeing the existence of one universal truth in all diversities found in the world. Therefore, a necessary step toward God-realization is to replace the world with God. Without changing one's worldview, one cannot transform one's attitude, and without the transformation of attitude, one cannot determine how to think properly. The history of spirituality reminds us that many great saints and devotees of God previously had been nonbelievers. Out of lack of knowledge, it is natural to remain indifferent toward the truth. Eventually, indifference may grow into nonbelief. In

the case of a fortunate one, however, indifference is removed, and curiosity to know the truth is born. Then, as he
searches, he finds. Once he finds, he can neither remain indifferent nor can he disbelieve any longer. In the Christian
tradition, St. Paul railed against Christianity, but later became a great devotee of God, and is now considered one of
the great saints of the West. In Indian history, the life of
Suradasa is a similar example of that kind of transformation.

Lacking in foresight, human beings consider their present
conditions and circumstances alone to be the truth. Taking
their present condition for granted, they refuse to explore
the possibility of other states of existence. The conscious
part of the mind fails to grasp that which lies beyond the
spheres of time, space, and causation. But another, more illumined, part of human consciousness is aware, at least sub-
liminally, that reality is more than what is known and seen.
Afraid to explore the unknown and unseen, most people
focus only on the existence of the manifest aspect of truth.
According to the scriptures, the unmanifest aspect of reality
is higher than the manifest world. Activities in the external
world are inspired and governed by the higher force of the
inner world. That which takes place in the physical world is
a mere reflection of that which has already taken place in the
inner world. The scriptures also state that the physical world
is governed by the force of the inner world. The nature of
inner life changes the quality of external life. The way we
think is the way in which we form our personality.

That inner world is also governed by an even more subtle
force of the Divine. From that unmanifest divine force, the
inner mental world evolves, and from there comes the external, physical world. Spirituality means allowing that inner
world to remain illumined by the light of the divine force. A

fully illumined inner world—which at an individual level is known as *chitta*, the mindfield—sends forth thought force into the external world. Even a ripple of thought arising from an illumined mindfield affects the external world. The thoughts, speech, and actions of illumined beings are in perfect harmony. They know they are citizens of two worlds simultaneously.

The purification and illumination of the inner world is of utmost importance. The mind, polluted by doubt, mistrust, and confusion, stands between divine awareness and physical existence. But the mind is the finest of all the instruments a human being has for exploring the truth within. Without proper thinking and discrimination, a human being fails to see his essential oneness with truth and therefore identifies himself with the external garment, the body. False identification with the body makes him a victim of pain and pleasure. His insatiable desire for pleasure and aversion to pain force him to keep transmigrating from one life state to another.

Believing in God also means believing in one's own godly nature. Without realizing his identity with God, a human being cannot attain peace and happiness. The belief that leads a human being toward immortality is the belief in God. That which leads him toward mortality is belief in untruth—that which is always changing, that which passes away.

After the purification of the intellect, faith in God is born. However, as faith is confined to the domain of the intellect, there is still questioning and doubt. A purified intellect is the most efficient tool for contemplation of the truth, but truth cannot be comprehended through the intellect alone. A sharp intellect can generate a hypothesis and, with the help of logic and reasoning, can prove it is true. But that intellectual hypothesis proven to be true may not necessarily be the truth. In fact, there is no end to such hypotheses, because there is no end to logic and reasoning. For example, the Nyaya system of Indian philosophy proves the existence of God through detailed logic and reasoning. In its profundity of logic, no other system of thought can stand against Nyaya, yet there are other philosophers who attack its logic and refute the existence of God simply by using another system of logic.

Usually an effect presupposes a cause, and almost every system of philosophy believes inference to be a valid source of knowledge. "Where there is smoke, there is also fire," one infers. There are philosophers, however, who are able to prove the fallacy of inferring the existence of a cause from a perceivable effect. Even the validity of knowledge based on direct perception can be contradicted by reasoning. A trained intellect can prove or disprove anything. However, whether the intellect validates or invalidates it, the truth itself is never affected. Truth is self-evident and self-existent. Logic and reasoning, if properly directed, can help the intellect turn inward to contemplate the inner reality, but the same process can also mislead the intellect, making it believe its own hypotheses instead of the truth. God is certainly not a subject of intellectual questioning and reasoning; otherwise the whole world could have realized God already. The intellect is of little value in experiencing truth directly, though it is a great instrument in discriminating between truth and untruth. Unfortunately, human beings do not have a better means than the intellect for contemplating within.

Brahman is the Lord of the universe. Pure existence, consciousness, and bliss are the intrinsic nature of Brahman.

The powers of creation, maintenance, and annihilation, the power to execute its own self-defined law, and the power to ignore or even nullify its own laws, are the inherent capacities of Brahman. Despite having all these powers and characteristics, Brahman itself can never be characterized, since all its powers are intrinsic to it, as heat is intrinsic to fire and light to the sun. Just as there is no difference between fire and its heat, or the sun and the sun's rays; there is no difference between Brahman and its inherent powers. They are one and the same. From the standpoint of unmanifest reality, Brahman alone exists, yet from the standpoint of manifest reality, the power of Brahman is also evident.

Although inseparable from Brahman, Shakti, the power of Brahman, is the cause of the creation, maintenance, and dissolution of the universe. The universe originates from Shakti, resides in Shakti, and is ultimately reabsorbed into Shakti. The one, single, nondual Shakti transforms herself into the vast universe. There is no Brahman apart from Shakti, and there is no Shakti apart from Brahman. Just as waves arise and subside in the water, the world of multiplicity appears, exists for a moment, and dissolves in Shakti. As water resides in the ocean, Shakti resides in Brahman.

The absolute truth, endowed with all powers and knowledge, is God. For an ignorant person, this universe is seen as different from God and therefore is considered to be illusory and unreal. For a wise person, however, this world is not different from God since there exists nothing but God. For such a person, all the powers and forces, even the material objects of the world, emanate from God, dwell in God, and function through God. Even the great divine forces known as *kala* (time) and *vidya* (knowledge), which control and maintain the entire universe, emanate from and function under the guidance of God.

The manifest world is pervaded by the subtle divine force. Like space, that force is abstract, expansive, and all-pervading. Without that force, nothing can exist and nothing can move. Just as our actions follow an inner inspiration, the movement of the cosmos follows the inspiration of the divine will. Whatever happens, whether in the microcosm or in the macrocosm, is inspired by the divine force which pervades all of the manifest and unmanifest reality.

Although the divine force is one, indivisible, and all-pervading, it assumes multifarious forms and names. In the manifest world, it transforms itself into energy and matter. Even modern physics accepts the transformation of matter into energy and vice versa. Merging with metaphysics, physics acknowledges the evolution of all known forces of the world from the more subtle force of an unknown reality. Modern physics has begun proposing the reality of an inexplicable but undeniable self-existent truth, which long ago was set forth in the Upanishads.

According to the Upanishads, the universe is an emanation of the divine force. All living and nonliving, moving and nonmoving, gross and subtle objects of the world are manifestations of the Divine. All the known forces of the world function under the guidance of that divine force. Sages of the past devoted their lives to the study of the subtle world and received direct experiences of divine illumination. Without relying on perception, inference, or postulation, without depending on physical tools and instruments, they penetrated the multileveled truth through their fully illumined and one-pointed intellect. The method through which they purified and trained their intellect is called sadhana, spiritual practice. Through practice, they reached a state wherein their entire being was illumined with the light of the Divine.

Before discussing the nature of Shakti, it is important to know the relationship between Shakti and the individual self. It is crucial to know how individuals are related to the universe, how an individual's inherent forces correspond with the forces of the cosmos, and ultimately how the individual's forces function independently yet in perfect harmony with the forces of the universe. Moreover, what is that force that tries to unveil this whole mystery of life, attempting to know itself? How do we decide we want to know the truth and what are the means to do so? According to the scriptures, the power of the will *(sankalpa shakti)* of the Divine is the answer to all these questions. Except for this power of will, there is no other means to experience the truth. The powers of knowledge and action are energized through the power of will. These and all other powers are inspired and guided by the power of will. The study of Shakti, therefore, necessarily includes the study of the powers of will, knowledge, and action, and their relationships.

Through the will of the supreme divine force, a human being is inspired to know the truth. Without the will of the Divine, all other forces in an individual remain inactive. By surrendering our desires to the will of the Divine, we find ourselves in the stream of divine consciousness.

All our actions and psychophysical functions can be divided into two main categories: voluntary and involuntary. Functions based on our desires, decisions, and determination are voluntary, whereas the functions that take place naturally and spontaneously are not governed by our willful determination and are called involuntary. Many bodily functions, such as blood circulation, heartbeat, and the contraction and expansion of the diaphragm and lungs, are involuntary. But through prolonged practice, a yogi can bring these involuntary functions under his conscious control. Through yogic disciplines, a yogi develops his power of will, and then through the power of will, he becomes master of his body. As he progresses with this discipline, he unveils the infinite field of his willpower and consequently attains mastery not only over his physical body, but also over his mind and the external world as well. At a certain stage in his sadhana, he experiences the oneness of the microcosm with the macrocosm. He realizes that his power of will is actually a power of the supreme divine force.

The ego stands between an individual and the Divine. By surrendering one's ego, one transcends the limitations imposed on the self, and consequently, one's power of will becomes one with the power of the divine force. Such a person attains perfection, since unrestricted power of will is at his disposal.

Living in ignorance, most individuals are not aware of their inherent infinite power of will. A greater part of their lives is governed by the force of nature. Humans are constantly driven by their instinctual urges, desires, whims, and fancies. Very rarely are they able to hear the voice of the heart and fully apply their willpower in carrying out their actions. Thus, they fail to put their whole heart into their actions and do not succeed. Their success and failure are governed by providence, which renders its judgment on the basis of a person's previous virtuous or nonvirtuous deeds. In the case of an accomplished yogi, however, the process of knowing, deciding, making an effort, and reaching the goal originates from and is governed by his unrestricted power of will. One must not forget that the unrestricted power of will of a yogi has become one with the divine will. Therefore it is not his will, but rather the will of the Divine, which inspires him to think, know, and achieve.

Human beings are still in the process of evolution. From birth to death, the power of will is being unfolded and that is called growth. In some human beings, that power unfolds itself much more rapidly and significantly, whereas in others it unfolds slowly and is barely noticeable. People with relatively more unfolded willpower are known as great, and those with a fully unfolded will are called perfect. The Upanishads declare: "The true self within cannot be known by those who are weak."

In the scriptures, the power of will is also known as the power of sovereignty. It is the self-illumined, self-guided power of consciousness. Because of that power, God is capable of creating, maintaining, and annihilating the universe. Without that force, one cannot even stir. By knowing the nature of that great force, a scientist can discover the cause of the universe. He can come to understand the fundamental force and its relationship with the manifest world. Such a scientist is a sage, a master of inner science. He knows the path that leads to the kingdom of eternity, immortality, and supreme bliss. Unfortunately, modern science still only explores the reality of the outside world and has paid no attention to the vast unknown inner part of reality.

Yoga and Vedanta, two related branches of Indian spiritual lore, offer a complete system to work on oneself, turn one's mind inward, and discover the forgotten truth within. By practicing yoga and contemplating Vedantic truth, we can study the truth right here in the laboratory of our lives. As we practice, our power of will unfolds. However, merely collecting information about yogic disciplines is not sufficient to allow one to experience truth directly. We have to commit ourselves to an uninterrupted, prolonged sadhana, sincerely and faithfully. The truth which resides inside cannot be seen by an outward-running mind. This inward journey is possible when we purify our intellect and make it one-pointed. Through a purified and sharpened intellect, we can understand the relationship between the power of will, the soul, and the external world. Once this mystery is solved, we come to know the wonders of the power of will. That which is ordinarily impossible becomes possible through willpower.

In all the great traditions of the world, the power of will is described as the prime and inherent force of God. According to both Eastern and Western traditions, God did not create this world as a potter creating pots out of clay. The omniscient, almighty, supreme Consciousness simply thought "Let there be a world" and there was a world; "Let me, the One, become many" and out of One, the world of multiplicity evolved. This indicates the unrestricted power of the will of God. In the history of Indian spirituality, one can find innumerable demonstrations of the power of will when great saints employed their yogic powers.

The law of karma also operates through the willpower of the Divine. The results of one's actions are presented to the performer of the action at the proper time. The willpower of the Divine arranges the fruits of one's actions in the form of samskaras, subtle impressions of past actions stored in the unconscious mind of the performer, until it is time for them to fructify in the form of external experiences.

The result we obtain today is a consequence of the kind of action we performed in the past. Similarly, the action we perform today determines the result we will get in the future. Usually there is such a long interval of time between the performance of an action and its result that we forget the causal relationship between the two. During that long interval, the causal relationship is maintained by the sam-skaras in our unconscious mind. The manner in which we think, speak, and act is imprinted on the vast screen of the unconscious. Later these unconscious impressions force us to think, speak, and act in such a way that we collect the fruits of our previous deeds. There cannot be a tree without a seed. And once the seed sprouts and grows into a tree, then usually there is no way to stop the tree from produc-ing innumerable similar seeds.

However, one must not become discouraged and must not stop the quest. The karmic process is entirely based on the action of the performer. In order to burn, fire has to be ignited. Once it is ignited, the fire can continue to burn only if someone adds fuel to it. Without a force which ignites a fire, the fire remains inactive or dormant and cannot burn at all. Similarly, the karmic fire and its capacity to burn have to be stimulated into action by a higher force. The supreme di-vine force is the prime factor igniting the karmic fire, and only after it is ignited does the rest of the process continue. Without the willful determination of God, a man born of flesh cannot move. Driven by the power of the divine will, human beings rotate the karmic wheel. Out of ignorance, false identification, and attachment, they consider them-selves the true performers of their actions and become caught in their self-created miseries. Because of their false identification, they impose limitations on themselves and don't know how to disentangle themselves. Because of their limited awareness, they fail to see the causal relationship be-tween their action and its fruit. Thus, driven by the law of providence, they helplessly taste the fruits of their actions. Liberation lies in knowing the will of the Divine, and realizing oneself to be an instrument in the hands of the Divine.

What else but God's supreme divine force can uphold this universe? What else can establish law and order, peace and harmony throughout this widespread diversity? The knowers of truth recognize that there is order throughout the universe. The sun, moon, stars, planets, and galaxies follow a law scientists call gravity. But they do not understand what causes that force. According to the Upanishads, behind all the forces such as electricity, gravity, light, and nuclear energy, there exists an indivisible, universal force which defines the nature of the world and its functioning energies. That indivisible, eternal, all-pervading existence is called consciousness. All that exists evolves from consciousness. Modern science is still confined to the study of matter and energy. So far, few have done any research on consciousness itself.

The study of consciousness is the study of the self. Consciousness cannot be studied through external means, and no other principle, aside from consciousness itself, can study consciousness. The laws and forces of nature are part of the power of the will of consciousness. All functioning energies of the universe manifest from the will of the Divine. In relation to the unmanifest Divine, the power of the will is one and universal, but in relation to the multiple manifest world, the power of the will is manifold.

The same is true with the powers of knowledge and action. In an individual, the basis for action is inner inspiration. If the inspiration is incomplete, impure, or has ignorance as its source, then the power of action fails to accomplish its intended task. Perfection in the power of action is entirely based on the purity of the power of will. Through constant purification one succeeds in removing the veil of ignorance. With the removal of this veil, the power of will comes forward and inspires the powers of knowledge and action. As a part of the spiritual journey from matter to soul, these three inner forces—the powers of will, knowledge, and action—work in accordance with one another. Consciousness carries on its eternal drama of descent toward the world and ascent back to its source. Through these three forces, consciousness alone becomes the material and efficient causes of creation, maintenance, and annihilation. Because of these inherent powers, consciousness, God, or truth is causally related to the manifest world, and at the same time remains transcendent.

Any object in the world has at least two factors as its cause. An object has a material cause, something other than itself, out of which it evolves into a particular form; the ancients called that principle the material cause of the object. For example, a pot is made of clay. However, without a potter the clay cannot shape itself into a pot or be fired in a kiln. Thus, the potter is the efficient cause of the pot. In order to organize, structure, or transform the material cause into an effect, the efficient cause must be self-conscious. It must have the power of will through which it can execute its powers of knowledge and action.

Through the power of will, which is the self-conscious, efficient cause, God wills the world to come into existence in a certain form. Through his inherent power of knowledge, he wills, and through the power of action, he materializes his will. In our worldly examples, there is nothing which can serve both as an efficient and material cause; an effect always has both a material and efficient cause distinct

connected by a common bond. Thus, each human being has his personal life, but by no means can he separate himself from his community, society, or humanity as a whole. His religion must offer peace and harmony in his personal, ethnic, and social life.

Community life sustained by high morals and ethical ideals can help one follow one's path with fewer conflicts and contradictions. Living in the world means responding to many duties simultaneously. Sometimes there may be conflict between assumed duties. In these situations, using discrimination, one must select the duty which provides for the welfare of a wider range of humanity. Whenever there is conflict between personal belief and universal values, one must choose the higher values of universal truth. One must learn to put aside all narrow-mindedness and become a part of the eternal kingdom. One must find a way to integrate one's personal goals and motives with the universal good of humanity.

Such a philosophy of moral standards, ethical formulas, and spiritual awareness of universal brotherhood constitutes the perennial religion of mankind. This is the universal religion of the Vedas and Upanishads, not today's sectarian dogmas and customs which create divisiveness and lead to conflict. Present-day religions must revitalize themselves by unfolding the inner streams of love, knowledge, generosity, courage, self-discipline, and forbearance as exemplified by the sages.

Religion does not flourish in history books, but in the lives of those who practice it sincerely. Religious people must live according to the high ideals and examples of their ancestors, rather than merely admiring and quoting their sayings. By understanding the basic values of the Vedic tradition, we can physically embody the true nature of religion. Unless we practice the essence of this noble heritage, there is no way to teach it to our children.

Women have the most important role to play in this task, for the mother is the child's first teacher. A mother's loving care and silent dialogue with her baby have the greatest impact on the young child's growth. Her moral and spiritual achievement is reflected in the upbringing of the child. At an early age, a child's curious mind and pure heart are very receptive. Children follow the footprints of their caretakers. They believe in whatever they encounter, regardless of whether it is right or wrong, good or bad. A mother who is emotionally mature can help structure the entire fabric of the child's life. She can inculcate in the child a foundation of self-acceptance and self-worth that will enable him to learn the principle of selfless giving. She can help her child understand that the life and objectives of other beings are never less significant than his own. She can make her child aware of the fact that his pleasures and pains are common to all children. When this awareness is cultivated in early childhood, it helps the child become an ideal citizen and upholder of higher values. Such children can become creative and useful members of society. Selflessness becomes part of their nature. This cannot be taught by teachers in school or preachers in temples; it is tacitly imparted only by mothers who themselves have gone through the process of self-transformation and self-discipline. Without this, there is no hope for significantly restructuring society.

The development of technology and communication media has made the world a smaller community where people from various ethnic groups have to coexist. To achieve peace and harmony, religions of the world must transcend their narrow outlook. They must strive to meet the ever-growing intellectual and spiritual needs of modern man. Today a system of rituals and ceremonial practices alone is not sufficient to fulfill our inherent desire to be happy here and hereafter. Followers of all religions must become open to the great comprehensiveness of their religion. Religion is based on the high ideals of humanitarian thinkers and realized sages with no place for narrow, parochial ideas.

Today, world religions have been divided into numerous sects and cults. The branches of these religions have become extremely rigid and thus have separated themselves from one another. But one must remember the true meaning of dharma as described in the scriptures. Dharma is that which leads humanity toward self-fulfillment. The perennial truths, rules, and laws which help maintain peace and harmony in one's individual and community life constitute dharma. Dharma applies for all times and in all places. It is the invisible force that helps individuals resolve their differences and thereby come closer to their fellow beings. Such a dharma and its meaning cannot be captured in the English term "religion." Any theory, principle, or policy that is not based on dharma is deficient, since it fails to offer a valid truth for all times and all places. Social laws and even national constitutions devoid of such dharma will lead a society toward inevitable decline.

The central theme of the Upanishads is "Brahman is real, and the transitory objects of the world are unreal." It teaches that Brahman alone exists and anything other than Brahman is illusory. Brahman is the source of life. Therefore, the highest goal of life lies in realizing the truth—Brahman. However, an exclusive emphasis on this doctrine can make one develop a negative attitude toward the world and

worldly relationships. Under the influence of such a doctrine, one might disregard worldly life. It is true that we
have an inherent desire to know ourselves, but at the same
time we are under the influence of temporal forces. The
sharing of thoughts and emotions with others is innate to
every human being. Keeping that in mind, the great sages of
the past set forth teachings that are helpful in balancing social, physical, mental, and spiritual demands.

Before following the disciplines of the revealed scriptures,
one must make an effort to understand the intent and effect
of these sayings by instilling in one's mind the concept that
Brahman alone is real and all else is illusion. This theory
helps an aspirant understand the true nature of material objects and how to use them as a means to attain the highest
goal of life. "The universe is unreal" means that we should
not get attached to the objects perceived by the senses; it
does not mean that we should disregard them if they are
helpful in achieving higher goals. It is impossible to attain a
desired goal without proper means. Material objects are
good as long as they are employed as a means, but they become a source of bondage the moment we consider them to
be the goal. Worldly resources become burdensome if they
are not used properly. Unless the transitoriness of worldly
objects is understood, we cannot leave trivial objects behind
and move forward. Without knowing the relative insignificance of the objects of the world, we cannot grasp the
higher truth, Brahman, which alone is real.

In the initial stages of sadhana, the theory that the empirical world is illusory helps one withdraw one's mind from
the external world and turn it inward toward the center of
life. At a later stage, when the aspirant has attained freedom
from the temptations of the world, he realizes that the

whole universe is an expression of Brahman. Then he no longer sees the difference between Brahman and the world. He does not need to separate himself from the world, for he perceives the world as part of his own being. This stage of spiritual evolution includes all and excludes none. Thus, there springs an eternal stream of love for all from his illumined heart. "This whole universe is Brahman" is the highest principle, whereas "The universe is unreal and Brahman alone is real" serves as a stepping-stone for experiencing the highest truth.

According to the Upanishads, an aspirant must analyze his spiritual growth so that he can practice those specific philosophical methods that are applicable to his present level of spiritual evolution. He must not misapply philosophical doctrines and spiritual practices belonging to different stages of life. A beginner who is still entangled in sensual pleasures begins by contemplating the philosophy that "the universe is unreal and Brahman alone is real." Only after a seeker has assimilated the wisdom of this first level should the next step be taken. Advanced seekers must not impose their conviction that "the universe is unreal" on those who have not yet learned the method of coping with worldly objects. An aspirant in his initial stage of sadhana need not renounce the world, but he must learn to utilize material objects creatively and skillfully. This means learning to use worldly objects as a means and not as an end. It is for this reason the scriptures insist that great men should live a lifestyle that is pure and simple on the one hand, and exemplary and practical on the other hand. It is not necessary for everyone to imitate each act of a great man. Only those acts that are applicable to the individual's personal growth should be adopted.

If we are to live in peace and happiness, every nation,

community, and individual must envision universal and humanitarian ideals and must strive to practice them in thought, speech, and action. Religion and even politics must be founded on moral and spiritual fundamentals. Politics and religion must not have power and control but the welfare of humanity as their goal. In ancient India, politics was regarded as a branch of ethics. It was not confined to legislation and rules of administration, rather it was open to exploration and experimentation in the light of truth. The laws were meant to make life less complicated. Peace, justice, and liberty for all were the prime purposes of politics. The objective of varied religions similarly helped ancient India to explore the possibilities of different paths to these ideals. The different branches of spiritual practice evolved not for the division of society, but as different approaches in the search for universal values and egalitarian ethics.

Spiritual life can be divided into two main paths: one advocates active involvement in worldly pursuits, and the other advocates renunciation. The first advocates karma yoga (selfless action) and the second proposes renunciation, which is actually self-conquest through self-sacrifice. In fact, both of these paths are inseparable. Without their complementarity, human fulfillment cannot be attained. By separating these two paths and adhering to one exclusively, we fight against ourselves and shatter the harmony of self, community, and society. A human being has a number of duties and obligations that cannot be fulfilled without worldly means and resources. However, a person engaged in worldly pursuits cannot have peace of mind because these worldly pleasures are not complete in themselves. Nevertheless, he cannot disregard them, for they are powerful enough to captivate the senses and mind. The path of renunciation, on the other hand, is not easy. It requires mastery over the senses and mind, a complete dispassion for worldly objects, and a burning desire for enlightenment. These characteristics cannot be acquired just by turning away from the world. They have to be cultivated through sincere practice, knowledge, and gradual transformation.

In society, conflict arises when the paths of karma yoga and renunciation are treated as separate. We forget that we have obligations toward others, and without completing these obligations, our renunciation is not valid. If everyone were to behave as if this universe is unreal without retaining a proper attitude toward the necessities of life, then society would collapse. Sometimes, out of spiritual immaturity, we ignore the basic values of human existence while we focus on this principle. We must strive to find the truth by conducting ourselves skillfully, lovingly, and selflessly. A dharma that fails to bring peace and harmony in personal and community life is no dharma at all. The perfection of dharma does not lie in personal achievement alone.

In order to achieve true happiness here and now, the physical aspects of life cannot be ignored. There is no need to consider the body unreal. With the help of a healthy body and worldly resources one can walk on the true path and practice meditation. Then, ultimately, with the help of the finest instrument—the mind—one attains liberation. In their proper context, the world and its objects are just as important as other subtle forces of nature. Nature bestows her wealth. The body and mind are instruments for both worldly enjoyment and spiritual enlightenment. Of course, in the context of Brahman, the highest truth, the body seems to be inferior and mortal. From another perspective, however, both body and soul are equally important and meaningful. The body is the means and Atman, the inner self, is the goal. Without the means, the goal cannot be achieved. Similarly, material objects are the means for the growth of society. Without adequate means and resources, community life cannot be happy and healthy. As community life and personal life are interrelated, it is necessary to maintain a balance between material and spiritual achievements.

Today, we need a religion which imparts equal importance to science and spirituality, material wealth and mental discipline. We need a religion that can guide humanity to achieve peace and happiness now and in the future. Such a religion would qualify to be the religion of all of us. That religion will help Hindus, Christians, Muslims, Buddhists, and Jews alike.

The word "dharma" has multiple meanings. According to some scholars, the performance of actions is dharma. According to others, actions upheld by righteousness alone are dharma. According to the Bhagavad Gita, karma or action has Brahman as its origin. This indicates that by performing actions rightly, one can attain Brahman. Any action can become a part of dharma so long as it is truth-oriented.

Having love for all human beings is dharma. Helping others ahead of one's personal gain is the dharma of those who follow the path of selfless service. Defending one's nation and society is the dharma of soldiers and warriors. In other words, any action, big or small, that is free from selfishness is part of dharma. However, the highest dharma is when one performs one's duties for the welfare of humanity lovingly and selflessly and, most of all, dedicates the action and its fruit to the Divine. One who has attained this highest form of dharma performs his duties in the world and yet remains above it. All his thoughts and actions become a part of dharma. His whole life is a field of dharma. He works hard without being attached to the fruits of his actions by offering everything to God.

The awakening of dharma can be initiated by proper education. Today's education, based on mere information, is incomplete. In modern educational systems, we are taught as many mundane things as possible, but this education does not offer any method for self-evaluation and inner exploration. Present education does not teach us how to make the best use of our heritage. Independent, critical thinking is not encouraged. That has resulted in leading people to confused and, at times, contradictory conceptions, and to then imitate one another blindly. As a result, some people erroneously believe that practicing a religion means either renouncing the world and chanting religious hymns and songs, or observing penances alone.

The Upanishads, however, do not advocate any of these ideas. In the Upanishads, we find universal dharma that includes both action and morality. These are the two great pillars on which the mansion of human virtues is erected. The goal of life can be attained by following a balanced path of discipline and righteousness. Such a dharma helps one live in peace and harmony. It inspires one to uphold justice and truth. It helps an aspirant attain the right goals through right means. The aspirant can help himself without harming others. Such a person can attain his personal goals and at the same time inspire others. His every action is directed toward defending dharma, supporting virtue, and inspiring others. The greatest scriptures, like the Vedas and Upanishads, set forth such an eternal dharma.

The intellect is superior to physical strength, but one must not forget that a sound mind dwells in a sound body.

The body and mind interact and influence each other, and become great instruments only if they work in harmony. As a means, they are of utmost importance in attaining the goal of life. Without proper means dharma cannot be defended. Shakti, strength, is the key factor in undertaking any project. Without this strength, human beings can neither uphold dharma, nor can dharma uphold human beings. Shakti implies mental and physical strength as well as worldly resources. The Upanishads repeatedly state "Live long and help others to live long."

The tradition of the Vedas was handed down by illumined seers and sages who realized the truth within. They did not simply think about religious values, but experienced them directly. Their direct experience is the foundation of their teaching.

There is a vast difference between a scholar and a sage. A scholar tries to understand the truth through the intellect, while a sage experiences it through a pure heart. A sage's direct experience is not based on sense perception or mental faculties. The information received through the intellect is like the waves rising on the surface of the ocean. On the other hand, true experience is received from the depth of the ocean of bliss, Atman. Truth lies not on the surface but in the depths of consciousness. Truth cannot be the object of mere perception; it is a matter of inner experience and a source of bliss. The illumined heart can easily experience what the intellect fails to grasp. Once there is direct realization, the door of knowledge opens forever and forms the basis of dharma. Philosophical debates, exhibitions of pedantry, and organizational drives cannot nourish the inner virtues of the perennial dharma.

Today, the human mind is afflicted with two miseries. On

the one hand, man suffers from materially-oriented social and cultural values. On the other hand, he has become a victim of fear and insecurity. Because of a materialistic attitude, modern man has an insatiable desire for worldly objects, which leads him away from the higher values of life, and he is burdened with religious dogmas that do not offer anything substantial to satisfy his intellectual search. Unfamiliar with the true significance of religion, he discards even the constructive and useful values of his religious heritage. Consequently, he turns into an atheist and disbeliever. He is not satisfied following dogmas and customs, but when he discards them in frustration, he is still dissatisfied. This dilemma has been created by blindly following teachers who themselves do not know what dharma is.

We must not be afraid to ask questions and find answers. We must not be afraid to discard illusion and embrace the truth. We must ask ourselves what good is that dharma which advises us to wander in the forest leaving our important responsibilities behind? What good is that dharma where there is no scope for correcting our mistakes in the world and living a clean and peaceful life?

Religion must meet its prime goal of loving all and excluding none. Certainly, religion must not allow any room for hatred and jealousy. Religion must lead humanity from diversity to unity; it must strive to remove inequality and distortions. Our society today has been shattered into pieces, and the innumerable existing religions have been instrumental in the process of its disintegration. We need valid concepts and self-discipline to help us transcend differences of opinion, contradictions in life, and odd complexes.

It is useless to brood on the past though; if possible, we should learn from the past. The journey of life cannot be completed by disassociating ourselves completely from past experiences. Past successes and failures remind us to stay on the right path and thus, if assimilated properly, the experiences of the past can make our present more constructive and creative. In the light of the past, we select the flower of the future. In order to brighten the future, the past is reborn in the form of the present. We must learn the art of remembering the past and creating a golden future simultaneously. Mere memory of the past resulting in worry, excitement, grief, or pride is worse than forgetting the past entirely. We must learn how to balance the past and the present to create a promising future.

As long as we are bound by superficial or dogmatic values from the past, we will not be able to reshape our present and guide our future. The blind faith, superstitions, customs, and dogmas found in our societies do not have their roots in the inspired scriptures. They do not have any rightful place in the vast body of eternal dharma. The seeds of hypocrisy, blind faith, and dogmas grow in the fertile soil of the self-centered proclamations of teachers who exploit the ignorance of their followers.

All teachers and preachers cannot be expected to have direct experience of the truth. If the custodians of religions and leaders of society had realized the truth, then the society and, for that matter, humanity itself would have been enlightened by now. Every human being subscribes to some belief or follows some religion. Every person has a teacher or a preacher or a precedent to guide him, and yet, the public-at-large is suffering from ignorance, inequality, and injustice.

With the passage of time, some day-to-day values of dharma have changed, but the parochial custodians of religion have not allowed a qualitative change to take place in society. Because of ego, narrow-mindedness, and selfishness, they fail to grasp a broader vision of reality. They lack the humanitarian spirit of religion. Instead of teaching universal truth, they propagate their personal beliefs. Afraid themselves, they discourage their followers from experimenting with new values to fit their ever-changing community life. The custodians of religion try to teach the scriptures in their own personal language and from their own peculiar perspectives. They exploit the humility and ignorance of their followers, who consider their exhortations to be the divine will. It is deplorable that their discourses are full of stories used to support their sectarian and tainted viewpoints. Behind the curtain of their discourses, there is little more than selfishness.

It is true that our ancient teachers were great, their wisdom was profound, their morals were high, and their spiritual insight transcended the limitations of time and place. However, we have not been able to take advantage of this great treasure that could have made life better and brighter. Instead, innocent people are told today that the exhortations of their preachers have the Divine as their source. They are forced to believe that the clergy are representatives of God, that their wishes are the wishes of God, and that they are the ones who should define the religious and moral standards of mankind. Such misconceptions have become the bane of the major religions of the world.

Dharma has been a great force in uplifting the human race. Dharma can help us today as it did in ancient times, but only if we start living the truth, not merely believing in it. Turning away from dharma and distancing ourselves from the truth is not a desirable way of living. It ultimately leads to misery. One who disregards dharma and ignores moral values remains confused. Such a person cannot have peace of mind. In the practice of dharma, one is advised to shed the veil of ignorance and practice truthfulness in one's thoughts, speech, and actions. How can dharma be secret, having revelation as its source? Withholding nothing, all the great sages in the world shared their knowledge with humanity. In the Bhagavad Gita, the Bible, the Koran, and the Dhammapada, knowledge, like the sun, shines for all.

Deceit leads to secrecy. The secret is that which cannot be presented to all. The elders say that there are only three places where we find secrets: in the life of an enemy, in the sectarianism of priests and preachers, and in selfish doctrine. Truth is a self-shining virtue. It is not meant to be fenced in and kept secret. The principles of dharma are eternal; they are enlivened with the power of truth. There is no need to shroud them under the veil of secrecy, and there is no need to teach those principles to the select few. Truth is open to all and so is dharma. Indeed, there are some spiritual disciplines that may be introduced only to those who are ready to practice them, but they are not reserved for any ethnic or privileged group. They are open to all sincere followers of dharma and are meaningful to those who can grasp their applicability and appropriateness.

Dharma resides not in dogma, rather it lives in the conduct of those who practice it. If we really believe in God, then that belief must pervade our thoughts, speech, and actions. It is hypocrisy to believe in high ideals but not practice them. Our day-to-day lives must be lived in accordance with our principles and ideals. There is no use in constructing a theory that cannot be applied in day-to-day life. A theory that is not practiced is no better than a body without breath. A principle or doctrine that can be practiced only in the temple or on certain occasions is hardly helpful for humanity at large. It is at best a fad that comes and goes.

To practice dharma, we must grasp the essence of all religions rather than merely be entertained by the fascinating stories retold by the preachers down through the ages. All the religions of the world have built castles of mythology. Preachers and priests recite myths as part of their worship and claim that listening to them is a source of spiritual enhancement. Assimilating the morals of those stories, rather than merely reacting to them emotionally, is the source of spiritual benefit.

A religious principle must have its roots in divine revelation. Religious doctrine originating from mere intellect is of little value. A doctrine that cannot uplift our souls, direct our thinking toward the Divine, and inspire us to act for the welfare of human beings should be questioned, analyzed, and reformed. In order to practice true dharma, one must surrender one's ego to the higher reality. One must transform one's thinking process and purify one's mind and heart. The purpose of dharma is to move closer to God by removing the wall of ego-born alienation. A follower of dharma strives to see truth, auspiciousness, and beauty in all living beings. That experience is called self-realization, enlightenment, or divine experience.

Today, in all religions of the world, the shining gems of truth have been shrouded under superstition, blind faith, and dogma. Human beings today are afflicted with a terrible sense of insecurity, fear, and mistrust. The dharma of the sages can help resolve these psychological and spiritual disturbances. The dharma of the sages is simple but experiential. However, people not committed to its practice and without living experience of its truths consider it to be mysterious. In fact, there is no mystery, no secrecy, in dharma. The mystery lies in our overly analytical minds, lost in complicated explanations which fail to grasp its profound simplicity. The dharma of the sages gives us a higher view of life which is not confined to the physical body or worldly objects alone. According to this dharma, we must rise above the charms and temptations of the world to employ our resources in the realization of the truth, the source of eternal peace. We must realize the truth in its totality and perfection.

Truth is more than the known and seen aspects of life. Truth exists in all times and places. Truth can be experienced within the depths of one's being. One can penetrate the various layers within and become one with truth through a systematic practice. Belief in truth is certainly better than disbelief, but it is the practice of truth that can transform one's belief into a creative and joyous experience. The sages who experienced and became one with the truth realized that all humanity is one family. According to the Upanishads, all of creation is a family. Spirituality enriched with humanitarian ethics is the inner breath of the Upanishads. Such high ideals are seldom practiced in any religion of the world. In the future, if humanity ever tries to establish a universal religion, it will be based on the profound teachings of the Upanishads. I long for the day when humanity will adhere to the higher principles of dharma.

According to the Upanishads, there is only one truth, called Brahman. Truth is omniscient and omnipresent. From a spiritual standpoint, the nondualistic statement "All this is Brahman" is not merely a philosophical doctrine; rather, it is a matter of experience. In addition, from an ethical standpoint, it provides a ground for cultivating an attitude of universal brotherhood. This statement helps one instill in one's mind the feeling that this whole world is a family. By considering all humanity to be one's own family, one rises above mutual differences.

In order to attain freedom and bring about peace and harmony in our society, we must respect only those principles based on direct experience of the truth. We must disregard doctrines that deter us from the path of enlightenment. No matter how charming and sweet a doctrine is, it is useless if it does not help us become more creative and useful for ourselves and for others.

There is no hope of attaining peace unless we start living a wholesome life. A wholesome lifestyle does not consist of becoming emotionally attached to the superficial values of religion. What difference does it make if we worship God wearing white clothes or red clothes? The real atheists are those who criticize others while claiming to be believers in God. Dharma is that which can be practiced by all and which can bring a qualitative change in individual and community life. Such a dharma is an eternal friend since it is always there in times of need. Such a dharma helps us attain the summum bonum of life both here and hereafter. It is the duty of mankind to practice and defend such a dharma, not the sectarian beliefs which create bitterness among human beings.

One may ask "What are the signs and symptoms of dharma?" The answer is "That which has no room for narrow-mindedness, sectarianism, blind faith, and dogma is the true dharma. That which has direct experience as its source, but welcomes logic and reasoning, is true dharma. A spiritual path that does not promise heaven only after death, but that helps the aspirant create a heavenly atmosphere wherever he is, is true dharma." One must not be afraid to follow such a dharma, or to absorb the higher qualities of universal dharma into his religious understanding.

Truth resides in those hearts where selfless love has found its way. True joy follows the center of love, and the purpose of life is to allow that love to flow throughout every aspect of life. When true love flows from the heart, one learns how to give and share without any expectation. Both the lover and the beloved are transformed through the force of love. In fact, selfless love and dharma are one and the same, since love is the inherent quality of the soul.

We become true followers of dharma when all of our activities are guided by truth and love. Ordinarily, people are not aware of the true nature of dharma but are caught in a net of religious knavery. Therefore, to ask them to reconsider and critically analyze the dogmas and practices of their religious traditions is upsetting. Many intellectuals of our society are not happy with their religious environment. However, they remain involved in so-called religious activities, for they haven't yet found an alternative. There is nothing wrong with the essence of any religion. The problems are created by preachers who claim to be custodians of the religion. Why there is so much contrast between theory and practice is a matter of serious consideration. It appears that to a great extent our present system of education is responsible for this problem.

Today, every human being tries to choose a lifestyle that pleases him. He wants to follow his own unique path. He disregards the wisdom of the past, and considers that disregard to be freedom of thought and freedom of conduct. Human beings are fond of experimenting with new values, modes of conduct, standards, and lifestyles, but these experiments lack a sound philosophical foundation. Consequently, the tendency is to move in diverse directions and arrive at conflicting conclusions. A human being should understand that his life must not be governed by selfishness and inactivity. No matter which kind of lifestyle he chooses, he must not allow antihumanitarian thoughts to invade his life. Most of humanity is practicing one religion or another, yet each person's worldview is confined to his own sectarian beliefs, customs, and dogmas. Ignorantly, one considers one's own convictions to be the highest religion, and fails to consider the welfare of humanity as a whole. The greatness of a religion is evaluated on the basis of the wealth and material objects possessed by its temples, churches, or clergy. Human beings are busy collecting the things that make them physically comfortable and enable them to lead luxurious lives. An unending desire for more has become the driving force of mankind.

Many members of our society have ignored the importance of divine dharma and as a result suffer from blind faith and dogmas. Almost every human being is religiously ill, and those who claim to be the healers of this disease are often even worse. Another segment of society focuses on technological achievements; they are trying to govern nature. They believe that nature will function under their command. Both groups have forgotten the underlying law of nature, the eternal law of truth. Both those who believe in a religion and those who do not, are equally distant from true dharma; neither is able to realize the purpose of human life. Neither has time to contemplate and decide which path to choose, which way to go, what to look for, and ultimately how to attain eternal peace.

For ages, our thinking processes have been modulated by a preexisting belief system that did not allow us to think independently. Relying on dogmas, human beings became weak. Through their own weakness, they accepted the superiority of blind customs, superstitions, and hypocrisy instead of dharma. With the passage of time they forgot dharma, replacing it with superficial norms and customs. This circumstance is more evident today than ever before.

According to the wise, knowledge alone is not enough. Knowing about dharma by itself may not lead one to work for the welfare of all. Sometimes great thinkers and idealists do not lead others to be productive. Such philosophers are absorbed in the process of thinking, considering thinking alone to be the highest form of dharma. They separate themselves from the rest of society and are unfamiliar with the needs and necessities of their fellow beings. Such thinkers therefore also fail to understand the current situation in their society. Thus, their teachings may be philosophically and doctrinally sound, but not very useful on a practical level. A thinker must maintain a universal attitude; he must think of the welfare of all and must examine the actual applicability of his theories. Only then will he succeed in offering the gems of true dharma to his contemporaries.

Some essential aspects of dharma:

1. Practicing dharma means maintaining God-consciousness through every activity in life. One accepts God as the supreme principle and allows one's individual life to be led in the light of God-consciousness. Accepting God means allowing truth and discrimination to guide all activities of life and consequently attaining freedom from selfishness, weakness, lack of discrimination, desire, and anger. The essence of dharma lies in practicing morality. The more we purify ourselves, the closer we move to dharma.

2. There is no need to teach a new dharma. Rather, the need is to purify one's life and make it truth-oriented. The method of purification must be in accordance with one's innate tendencies and inner inclinations. Dharma consists of making oneself pure in thoughts, speech, and actions. Cleanliness, contentment, and morality are the signs of adhering to dharma.

3. Dharma should be practiced in every aspect of life. The highest good lies in reaching the center of one's being, Atman, and finally experiencing the oneness of Atman and the supreme truth, Brahman. In order to attain the highest good, one passes through various stages of spiritual awareness. First, the seeker attains knowledge. Through constant practice and contemplation, the knowledge is assimilated and then becomes an inseparable part of one's being. The strength gained through knowledge helps one overcome blind faith and dogmas. One attains pure faith and surrenders oneself to the divine force, once and forever.

4. Dharma protects the individual, as well as societies, whenever materialism tries to swallow humanity in its ever-growing thirst for the accumulation of worldly riches. Therefore, only ethics and politics based on dharma can be beneficial for human growth.

5. Today politics has separated itself from dharma and thereby has created chaos in our society. We must uplift ourselves; we must not allow human values to be undermined. This is possible only if we can bring dharma into our day-to-day lives.

6. Dharma protects human beings from becoming lost in the material world. It reminds the aspirants of the importance of spiritual life by pointing out the transitory nature of the objects of the world and the sense pleasure derived from them. With the decline of dharma, the ugly forces of

selfishness, egoism, violence, prejudice, and discrimination invade our minds and hearts. Do not let those demonic forces plunder your peace of mind and hinder your growth.

7. Dharma means discovering love, truth, and peace in one's life, and these discoveries contribute to the fulfillment of all individuals as well as to humanity as a whole. It is good to contemplate the Divine, but living the life of a philosopher, while escaping from one's duties and wandering hither and thither without organizing one's life, cannot be condoned. Such researchers of the truth contribute nothing to the welfare of others. The practice of dharma begins with one's individual life but ends in the collective life of all mankind. An aspirant withdraws himself from worldly affairs not as an escape but rather with the intention of managing his time and energy for higher achievements. Once he achieves this, he goes back to the world and shares the fruits of his achievement with the rest of humanity.

8. The sense of security is the mother of peace. Human beings cannot achieve security by competing for material wealth or by running after endless successes in the fields of science and technology. For true security and peace of mind, we have to attain mastery over ourselves.

9. The awareness of dharma comes from the realization that the stream of life is not confined to the tiny part of our being we know so far. The stream of life originates from the Divine, which is higher than, and superior to, human life. By realizing this truth, a sincere seeker of dharma casts off his ego and begins experiencing the oneness of the life force within all living beings. Such an aspirant never considers any sectarian belief to be of higher authority than the truth.

10. Today, we need a path of discipline to help us maintain the peace and happiness usually compromised by dis-

ease, old age, and the fear of death. A path that helps us remain unperturbed by such afflictions is the dharma of mankind. Only such a dharma can help us live in the world and yet remain unaffected by suffering and loss.

11. There was a time when the sentiment "This is mine, and that is yours" was an attitude of those with little minds. For a person with high character and a broad mind, this whole world is a family. Such a humanitarian and egalitarian attitude is the ethical aspect of dharma, whereas the direct experience of nondual truth is the spiritual foundation of the perennial dharma. Whenever humanity is ready to set forth a universal religion, it will have to return to the gems of truth from the Vedas and Upanishads, which long ago declared "The whole world is one family."

12. Dharma is pure in itself. The purity of dharma cannot be compromised with sectarianism. A sectarian religion is open to a limited group of people whereas dharma embraces all and excludes none.

CHAPTER THREE

SPIRITUAL PRACTICE

A HUMAN BEING IS BORN into a family and assimilates the elements of the family environment as he or she grows up. Because one's early environment has such an enormous impact on every child's development, the family must lay the foundation for social reformation and for spiritual enlightenment. Without a solid family institution, the means and resources to grow either in the external or spiritual worlds cannot come together. When all the members of the family have one objective and work together with full cooperation, they reach their goal with fewer distractions and impediments. Such an ideal family is a perfect training center where every member learns the art of living a happy life. However, there cannot be such an ideal family unless people devote part of their time to spiritual practices.

From the beginning of history, human beings have aspired to be perfect. The desire for perfection led them to study the various aspects of life. In most cases, they studied the external world and tried to achieve peace and happiness through worldly objects. Then, they realized that no matter how many objects they had, they remained dissatisfied. In spite of all the things at their disposal, they still felt unfulfilled. According to the Upanishads, everlasting fulfillment lies in attaining perfection within. Inner perfection can be achieved by rising above self-imposed limitations and by knowing the true nature of Atman, which is eternal, omniscient, and free from all limitations. The sages of the Upanishads prayed to God not for worldly pleasures, but for spiritual enlightenment. The famous prayer found in the Upanishads, "Lead me from the unreal to the real, lead me from darkness to light, lead me from mortality to immortality," reflects the innate longing of all human beings. For thousands of years, people have employed their bodies, senses, minds, and intellects to explore the subtleties of life as it relates to the external world, yet so far they have not yet achieved freedom from fear and insecurity. Unfortunately, their search has remained partial, for they did not study a large part of their being—the mind and self. Fulfillment lies in creating a balance between spiritual and worldly life. Creating harmony between these two aspects of life is called sadhana, spiritual practice.

For spiritual practice, a person does not have to separate himself from his family, relatives or society. He cannot and need not renounce anything at all, since nothing belongs to him anyway. Desire for renunciation of worldly possessions is an indication of his ego and ignorance. The objects of the world belong to God and are meant to be used as a means for knowing God. As long as one uses worldly objects as a means to achieve higher goals, one does not get attached to them. Those who understand the principles of nonattachment and practice them in their day-to-day lives attain freedom here and now. Renunciation of worldly objects is not as important as enjoying them without becoming attached to them. According to the Upanishads and the Bhagavad Gita, renunciation means to live in the world, yet remain above it.

To attain perfection here and now, one must undertake some spiritual discipline, for without practice one cannot attain control over the modifications of the mind. Unless the mind is made one-pointed, an aspirant cannot unfold his inner potentials. The mind is the cause of both bondage and liberation. A one-pointed mind can help one go within and unveil the mystery of inner life, whereas an undisciplined mind remains dissipated, and thus fails to grasp the true nature of worldly objects. An outwardly oriented mind runs from one object to another, hoping to find peace and happiness in the external world. Lacking inner awareness, the mind refuses the guidance and inspiration of the subtle divine force. A mind which is not guided by divine illumination stands like a wall between the aspirant and his goal. Having such a mind, a person fails to study the inner dimensions of his life, and as a result considers this external world alone to be the sole reality.

When we look at our lifestyles, we find that we are not making the best use of our time and energy. A precious part of our lives is wasted in meaningless activities. There is a close relationship between spiritual practice and proper timing. Without regularity it is not possible to transcend one's habit patterns or transform one's personality.

For any practice, an aspirant also needs a strong, healthy body. When he regularly practices one sitting posture for a prolonged period of time, his body becomes still as a result.

Then he realizes that although he has a body, he is not the body. At the same time he knows that the body is a great instrument and that he should take care of it properly. An unhealthy body dissipates the mind, for most of his energy is then directed to the body alone. A person with an unhealthy body does not have time to work on other aspects of his being. Thus, physical health is considered to be an essential part of spiritual practice.

When he sits comfortably in his meditative posture and his body is still, the aspirant observes the impact of his *prana,* life energy, on his body. Physical activities are based on the functions of pranic energy. Breath is a barometer to measure one's inner state. By practicing yogic breathing exercises, one attains balance between inhalation and exhalation. Regulation of inhalation and exhalation helps one to still one's body and mind. Just as a fresh, nutritious meal is necessary for the body to function, we also require fresh, clean air. At least three times a day, an aspirant should practice some simple breathing exercises. While keeping his head, neck, and trunk straight, he should sit comfortably and do deep diaphragmatic breathing. By regulating his breath, he can easily attain control of the modifications of his mind.

Unsteadiness of body and breath are a chief source of mental distraction. Once these distractions are removed, an aspirant succeeds in attaining control of the thought waves in the mind. The more the mind is made steady and one-pointed, the more one experiences peace and happiness within. There are several ways of making the mind steady and one-pointed. Among them, concentrating on one's breath is considered to be the best. One should pay attention to the breathing and make sure that there is no unevenness and no noise during inhalation or exhalation. The aspirant should breathe deeply, diaphragmatically, and without a pause between the inhalation and exhalation. Concentration on the flow of breath is one of the best ways to attain control over the modifications of the mind. When all the modifications cease, and the mind is calm and tranquil, one finds great joy within. When the mind is free from all distractions, and starts traveling inward, the aspirant begins to unveil the mystery of the multileveled reality. Through his one-pointed mind, he gains knowledge of the inner world, which is more reliable than the knowledge derived from perception, inference, or testimony.

In the initial stages of meditation, a student learns to calm his conscious mind. He withdraws his attention from the external world and focuses it on an internal object. When the conscious part of his mind is relaxed, he notices a train of thoughts disturbing his inner tranquillity. At that moment, the student should remain firm and should not identify himself with those past impressions. He should pay full attention to the object of concentration, which will help him remain uninvolved with memories which spontaneously arise. Gradually, he crosses that phase and starts experiencing the unalloyed truth. The experience of the truth is pure in itself. When an aspirant has understood the conscious part of his mind, and thereby attained mastery over it, he naturally performs his actions skillfully and efficiently. Compared to the unconscious, the conscious part of the mind is very small. However, there is close interaction between the unconscious and conscious minds. Once an aspirant has attained freedom from the distractions originating in the conscious part of the mind, he can have a better grasp of the thought constructs that originate from the unconscious mind. Through his undisturbed, prolonged practice, a student dives deep and becomes familiar with his inherent potentials. He observes how the experiences of the external world are a mere reflection of his inner world.

Human beings inherit a vast treasure of knowledge. They can have access to that treasure only if the mind is made one-pointed and inward. Beyond the mind, there is the intellect. The power of the intellect guides the functions of the mind. When the mind is purified, distractions are removed, and thereby one-pointedness is gained. Such a mind then begins following the guidance of the intellect. Unlike the mind, which always remains in a state of doubt, the intellect is endowed with the power of discrimination and decision. The mind, fully guided by the higher faculty of the intellect, becomes a great instrument to achieve peace and happiness. However, one should remember that a dissipated mind is too unfocused to listen to the voice of the intellect. The intellect guides only the one-pointed mind. Therefore, the most important step in spiritual practice is to make the mind one-pointed so that it can be guided by the decisive faculty called the intellect. The method of making the mind one-pointed is called meditation. Through meditation, an aspirant withdraws his mind from the external world, focuses on a given internal object, and develops an interest in delving within.

As meditation matures, the mind becomes one-pointed and its modifications are removed. Such a tranquil mind begins working in accordance with the intellect. No contradiction remains between the functions of the mind and intellect. Usually, the impurities of the mind such as doubt and conflict pollute the intellect, but through meditation these pollutants are removed from the mindfield. Thus, the intellect is not disturbed by the activities of the mind, and the meditator experiences an extraordinary peace within. The intellect is described in the scriptures as a mirror that is in the closest proximity to Atman. As long as the mirror of the intellect is clean, it reflects the clearest and least distorted vision of Atman. If the intellect is colored with the thoughts and feelings of the lower mind, it presents a distorted picture of Atman. Therefore, according to the Upanishads, one should remove all impurities from the mind, and make the mind free from all doubts and conflicts, so that the intellect can be as pure as crystal. An intellect free from the influences of the lower mind finds itself in a well-balanced state. Only such an intellect is capable of making an aspirant self-confident and self-reliant. Gaining such an intellect, the meditator knows the goal of life is not far away.

An intellect free from the disturbances of the lower mind attains the illumination of Atman from above. Darkness belonging to the realms of the mind and senses cannot exist in the light of an illumined intellect. In the absence of all thought constructs, the lower mind merges into the intellect. When the intellect is absorbed into the divine light, that is the state of *samadhi*, the state of fearlessness and immortality. As long as a human being takes refuge in worldly objects, the body, pranic energy, and the forces of the lower mind, he remains a victim of old age, death, and rebirth. But when the intellect is fully illuminated by the light of Atman, he is fearless. At the dawn of spiritual enlightenment, the mind and intellect find their place in the kingdom of Atman, and one thereby attains freedom from the pairs of opposites such as pain and pleasure, heat and cold, good and bad. This is the highest state of freedom. One who dwells in the domain of Atman does not belong to a particular family, society, or nation. Rather, he is part of all of humanity. He loves the welfare of all as much as he loves his own self.

The joy derived from samadhi, spiritual absorption, is indescribable. No sense pleasure can be compared to it. One who has reached the state of samadhi shares his joy with all humanity. He is like the sun that cannot be kept in darkness. Since wisdom and compassion are the essential outcomes of samadhi, he follows the path of selflessness in his thoughts, speech, and actions. Selfless service is a common characteristic of all great souls. It is also the way to purify one's heart and walk on the path of enlightenment. Our society needs aspirants who are selfless and fearless and who consider service to be part of their sadhana.

One should be aware of the goal of life and make sure that one is not wasting precious time. Those who practice sincerely reach the goal. If someone is blessed with divine grace and commits himself to spiritual practices at an early age, one day, no doubt, he will accomplish his goal. For practice done in childhood becomes a foundation for one's whole life. A child has not yet assimilated much of the world in his mind; with very little effort he can have control over his mind. However, those who did not have such an opportunity in their childhood should not feel discouraged. It is never too late to begin spiritual practices. One can begin in childhood, youth, adulthood, or old age, and still become accomplished. Through practice anyone can be transformed. Practice helps one change habit patterns and form new and spiritually conducive habits. After practicing for a long time, regularly, and without interruption, practice becomes a part of one's being. Then the aspirant moves toward the goal effortlessly. That is the highest form of practice, described in the scriptures as "effortless effort."

Before committing himself to any practice, a student should design a schedule of discipline he will be able to follow easily. Self-discipline helps him cultivate his willpower and determination, with the help of which he can accomplish any task. The attitude "I can do it, and certainly I will do it!" helps one control the modifications of the mind. The mind, free from modifications, naturally becomes one-pointed and strong. At the very beginning of one's spiritual journey, one should not attempt too many or overly intense disciplines. In failing to follow one's self-designed resolutions, one impairs one's willpower. One should not allow willpower to be polluted by the weakness of the mind. It is the nature of the mind to resist discipline. Sometimes students are dismayed by this tendency of the mind and lose confidence in themselves. The moment they feel they are not capable of accomplishing the desired goal, they become victims of hopelessness. Hopelessness affects willpower adversely, and as a result, resolutions are postponed. All this happens because of the mind. Therefore, the mind is the most crucial factor in spiritual practice.

After morning ablutions, one should do some yogic exercises. Exercise should be practiced according to one's capacity. Yogic postures are better than all other exercises. They ensure not only physical but also mental health. With the practice of yogic postures, the body overcomes laziness and becomes strong and energetic. However, it is important to be moderate while practicing yogic exercises. How much exercise one should do depends on one's physical capacity and age.

After the exercises, the aspirant should learn how to sit still in one of the meditative postures. He should select one of the sitting postures and should not change that posture often. It is good to master just one posture—one he finds to be comfortable and steady. All sitting postures which keep the head, neck, and spinal column aligned are good. If one sits regularly in a meditative posture, he will reduce any tension and stress on his cardiovascular system. The place where he sits should be neither too hard nor too soft. He can make a cushion by folding a woolen blanket a few times.

If the body is not comfortable and steady, then certainly it creates a disturbance in the mind. Without one-pointedness of the mind, meditation or repetition of mantra is not very fruitful. If the sitting posture is applied properly, the body becomes free from all aches, pains, and jerks. By sitting still in one posture even for ten minutes, one can observe the benefit of stillness. That experience is entirely different from the experience of seeking worldly objects. When inhalation and exhalation move evenly without a jerk or pause, then the mind naturally turns inward. A mind free from the distractions of body and breath becomes one-pointed and inward. After making his body comfortable and steady in one of the sitting postures, the student should pay attention to the next step of the practice.

The next step consists of opening *sushumna* so that the upward journey of the mind through the sushumna channel can begin. According to the yogic scriptures, there are 72,000 *nadis,* energy channels. Among them, *ida, pingala,* and sushumna are the most important. Usually prana (the life energy) and the mind travel through ida and pingala, supporting all of our psychophysical activities. As long as the mind is directed outward, only the two side channels, ida and pingala, remain active. But when the mind is calm and tranquil, sushumna, the central channel, is awakened. The joy derived from the mind traveling through the sushumna channel is unique; it cannot be compared with any sensory pleasure. Because of that inner joy, the mind loses its taste for worldly objects. According to yoga manuals, sushumna application is the most important factor in spiritual practice. The moment sushumna is awakened, the mind longs to enter the inner world. That is called true awakening. When the flow of ida and pingala is directed toward sushumna, and distractions are thereby removed, meditation flows by itself. The mind slips into a state of meditation and attains freedom from all the *vasanas* (mental modifications) and samskaras. Sushumna application is a great step, but mastering the process requires practice.

After sushumna application, one progresses to the next stage of spiritual awareness. A great force resides within all human beings. The purpose of sadhana is to experience that force. Except for the realized sages, that force remains dormant in all human beings. In the scriptures that force is known as the power of Atman, the power of God, or the divine force. Just a fraction of that awakened divine force is capable of changing the course of one's life. At the awakening of that force, one is blessed with intuitive revelation. Through their profound contemplation and meditation, the sages of the Upanishads awakened this force and attained knowledge of the absolute reality.

However, there are aspirants who practice meditation for a long time and still cannot awaken that force. There are three reasons why they fail:

1. The wrong method of meditation.
2. Irregularity of food and exercise.
3. Irregularity in the practice itself.

If someone practices properly, there is no reason for not awakening that force. Once awakened, it leads one to the state of samadhi, the state of self-realization. The moment that force reaches the center of consciousness, the blessed aspirant attains all the *siddhis,* the supernatural powers. Such an aspirant is an adept who remains in perfect union with the supreme consciousness.

Sometimes people ask whether that practice is possible in our times, how much time is required to do such practices, and how one can practice such disciplines while living in the world. These are natural questions that arise in seekers' minds. The wise ones reply to these questions clearly and succinctly: "No matter which practice one does, one has to discipline oneself. A human being is fully equipped with all the powers and capacities to gain the knowledge of the truth. He needs to organize himself and make the best use of his inherent resources."

People have made themselves needlessly busy. They should learn to make better use of their time. Because of their hectic lifestyles, people are suffering from tension and stress. They create a need for worldly objects, then they busy themselves in meeting that need. A great part of their lives is consumed in collecting worldly objects, and very little time is left to enjoy them. Managing one's time is the most important task on the path of spirituality.

Students need to discipline their four innate urges: food, sleep, sex, and self-preservation. These four urges are constantly subduing our inner strength. If not regulated, these primitive urges can create a great impediment to one's practice. A large part of spiritual practice consists of the rules and disciplines that help regulate these four natural drives. In addition, one should be punctual in sleeping and arising, perform one's daily duties lovingly and one-pointedly, enjoy objects moderately, and not allow feelings of fear or insecurity to occupy the mind.

People of the modern world want to enjoy material things, but are incapable of doing so. Due to lack of discipline, they have lost the capacity to enjoy the objects of the senses. Before they have attained these objects, while they have them at hand, and after they have lost them, they experience nothing but pain. A human being desires pleasure but receives pain. What a miserable life! Happiness does not reside in the objects of the senses, but rather in that eternal divine force that supports the mind and the senses. Through discipline and determination, one can awaken one's inner strength or willpower. Through one's willpower one can discipline the primitive urges: food, sleep, sex, and self-preservation. Once these are regulated, an aspirant does not have any resistance to practices. He enjoys a disciplined life; waking up on time, doing exercises, practicing pranayama, and meditating become a part of his being. He attains success in any task he undertakes.

An aspirant does not need to disrupt his worldly life to practice spirituality. However, he must not waste time only in material pursuits. The key point is to manage his time and energy so he can have the worldly resources that are necessary for a comfortable life. At the same time, he should be able to devote himself to spiritual pursuits. He should understand how fear invites catastrophes into his life; how excessive sleep leads to inertia and laziness; and how indulgence in sensory pleasures drains physical and mental energy. Running after sensory pleasures, desire grows, but an aspirant's energy level goes down. He should learn to enjoy things at their proper time and place. The method of enjoyment should also be wholesome, so that he does not become a victim of enjoyment itself. By practicing the following instructions from the Bhagavad Gita, an aspirant can create a harmonious balance between the external and internal aspects of life: "Yoga, spiritual practice, helps the practitioner transcend all pains and miseries only if he is moderate in food, in physical and mental activities, and if he sleeps and awakes on time."

Chapter Four

Turning Over a New Leaf

A HUMAN BEING HAS A BODY, but he is not the body. He is pure, eternal consciousness. He must not spend all of his time running after physical pleasures. He should search for his true identity and accomplish the highest goal of life. The purpose of having a body and mind is fulfilled only if they are used as a means to the highest goal. Neither the body nor mind can be the center of life since they are meant for something other than themselves. Once we contemplate within, we realize that the body, mind, breath, and senses are serving a master who is not yet known. Who can that master be? According to the scriptures, after knowing that master within, nothing else remains to be known. After realizing that master, one becomes immortal and invincible. That master is the Atman, pure consciousness. A person aspiring to know Atman must first learn how to use worldly resources properly and skillfully. Objects of the world must not become the goals of life. They are a means, and without proper means there is no way to attain the goal.

The basic purpose of a religion or spiritual path is to help humanity attain self-realization. Religions are composed mostly of philosophy, mythology, rituals, codes of conduct, and social laws. All of these are meant to establish a balance among the various aspects of life. An aspirant must understand that these are components of, not the goals of, religion. They are the means for instilling virtues in his mind and heart. Then he can easily simplify the various aspects of his life and can devote a greater part of his time and energy to knowing the truth. That is the goal of all religions. In most cases, people take pains for the means and forget the goal. The various religions of the world have employed different means to reach the goal, and thus, from the standpoint of the means, one religion seems to be different from another. From the standpoint of the goal, however, all religions lead to one single truth.

Rigidity and narrow-mindedness are the most injurious elements for both a religion and religious people. Except for the Upanishads, no single scripture proposes the principles of a universal dharma. The teachings of the Upanishads are more valid than other scriptures because in the Upanishads there is a perfect balance between intellect and direct realization. The Upanishads give priority to revelation, but never discourage intellectual inquiry. According to the Upanishads, religious doctrines must be questioned, and if they are found to be intellectually satisfactory, only then they should be practiced. In the practice of true dharma, as the Upanishads advise, one should not become complacent. One must not be satisfied only with one's intellectual knowledge of dharma. Experience alone can make one confident of what one knows. A person with perfect balance between his intellectual knowledge and direct experience can be a true teacher of dharma.

A teacher without experience cannot guide humanity in the right direction. His teachings are based on the information received from books or from other teachers. An inexperienced teacher fails to recognize the needs of contemporary society, and regardless of its applicability, he teaches what others taught in the past. There is a strange custom in many countries; anyone born in a teacher's family automatically becomes a teacher. Such teachers simply follow the old customs, perform time-honored ceremonies, and offer discourses with the intention of impressing their audience. Lacking in practice and discipline, they are perfunctory preachers. Their writings and speeches lack foresight. Instead of establishing peace, harmony, love, and universal brotherhood, these teachers encourage jealousy, hatred, differences, and group identities. It is because of these preachers that our society now suffers. Although the Upanishads teach the philosophy of nondualism, people continue to condemn each other.

According to nondualistic philosophy, there exists only one Brahman. One single truth manifests in the form of the universe. Therefore, all creation is a manifestation of God. Every individual is a living shrine of God. No one is inferior; no one is superior. In order to reinstill these values, we need to revolutionize our system of education. Education should improve general awareness; it should touch every niche of society.

This is the time to go back to the original scriptures of the Upanishads and the Vedas, although we do not need to follow all of the instructions found in them unless they are proven to be helpful for our growth. It is written in the

Vedas, "Follow only that part of the teaching which is help-ful to your present level of evolution, and leave the rest for future exploration." This Vedic statement clearly indicates that the wisdom of the sages is not meant for a particular community. It also indicates that the truth is one, but it has been presented in various gradations and degrees. The goal is one, the paths may be many. Likewise God is one, al-though his forms may be many. People have the freedom to select any of these forms for meditation and worship, but the ultimate goal is to realize the formless, nameless, ab-solute truth.

It is wrong to evaluate the performance of one religion in comparison to another. There are differences in approach, but that does not mean one religion is inferior or superior to another. However, there is one essential quality for a gen-uine religion, and that is loving all and excluding none. A re-ligion that incites its followers to hate others is not a religion at all. Such a religion is actually a man-made creed and has nothing to do with the divine will. That self-centered and rigid "religion" is injurious to human growth. In this age of high technology, in which people are continually interacting and evolving, there is no room for sectarian rigidity. It is sad that humanity is still divided; people are still imposing their narrow and rigid viewpoints on one another. They have not yet found a universal religion.

God is the goal of all religions, yet one religious school differs from another. Is one religion expounded by God while another is not? Does God really prefer one religious approach to another? The answer is an emphatic "No!" The differences are a result of religious organizations. This orga-nizational attitude forces people to separate themselves from one another. Eventually, differences arise even among the members of the same organization, and thus they split, branching out into different sects. Such an attitude is actually antireligious; it compromises the purity and dignity of a given tradition.

The basic principles of all religions are universal. The welfare of all mankind is a prime goal. Out of ignorance, people identify a religion by its method of worship, prayers, and ritualistic activities. Unfortunately, they focus undue attention on the methodology itself, and forget the actual intent of worship and prayers. These methods gradually lead to customs and dogmas, and a religion is replaced by rigidity, narrow-mindedness, and superstition. What difference does it make if we wear mala beads or a cross around our necks, or whether we recite prayers in Sanskrit, Arabic, or English? Yet these are the types of issues over which adherents of religion fight. There is no reason for two religious groups to fight with one another over truth, because the truth is one. A person believing in an eternal truth cannot confine himself to mere customs and dogmas. A researcher of truth should never criticize a religious tradition to which he does not belong. He should know that all religious traditions have been set forth by enlightened sages. His lack of knowledge of another religion should never undermine the greatness of that religion.

In its truest essence, every religion professes the existence of an unmanifest, supreme divine force. However, it also professes an anthropomorphic image of the Divine as a stepping stone to the absolute reality. Anthropomorphism evolved as an attempt to capture the infinite in finite terms. Finite symbols and images are diverse. Due to their specific backgrounds, inner tendencies, and interests, people prefer a certain image and ignore others. From such inclinations, differences arise in the way people of different religions visualize their deity. Another cause of religious diversity is the worship of religious leaders. People gather around a great man; gradually his following grows, and one day, his teachings are established as a separate religion. Such tendencies and practices do not allow humanity to search for truth without prejudice.

The wisdom of the Upanishads can help us glimpse universal truth. It can show us a path leading to the realization of absolute reality. The Upanishads generally do not advise an aspirant to become involved in the worship of any personified god or goddess. And when they do, first they explain the philosophical and spiritual significance of the symbolism. Knowing the inner significance of a symbol or image of God, a person worships the image as a means to attain the truth signified by it. As soon as the purpose is accomplished, he moves ahead, leaving the symbolic worship behind. While he is worshiping a particular image of God, he knows that the particular image is neither inferior nor superior to other images. He also knows that such methods of worship are only means to channel his thoughts and emotions toward God. Once he rises above symbolism and attains a direct experience of the absolute truth, he abandons such practices once and for all.

Without self-realization, a human being wanders about in vain. He remains insecure and fearful. On the one hand, he finds himself completely lost, on the other hand, he feels that something is inspiring him to find his way and attain freedom. Because of a lack of confidence, willpower, and determination, he fails to respond to the voice in his heart. Out of many, only a few decide to walk on the path of freedom, and they are called the awakened ones. Their will and inner strength determine how far and how quickly they will move toward the goal. The awakened ones try their best to follow the path of light. But soon they face a great hurdle which cannot be overcome through any external means or through the intellect.

The intellect is the finest instrument a human being has for the inward journey, but the intellect has its limitations. The intellect cannot grasp nondual, pure consciousness. The intellect perceives things as objects. Its power to perceive, analyze, and discriminate is due to the power of divine will. The intellect functions in the objective world. Beyond the objective world exists pure consciousness, which cannot be perceived or experienced by anything other than consciousness itself. However, the intellect must be purified so that it can discriminate right from wrong and the good from the pleasant.

The power of discrimination or right discernment shines through a purified intellect. While living in the world, one can make one's life less complicated by proper discernment. However, in the spiritual realm, direct experience alone can be one's guide. A human being simultaneously lives in both worlds, external and spiritual. For his all-around growth and happiness, he needs a balance between intellectual knowledge and direct spiritual experience. It is advisable for a human being to allow his external activities to be guided by spiritual insight. Spiritual insight, direct realization, revelation, and intuitive awareness are different terms to express the same truth. Self-realization means the unfoldment and expansion of higher consciousness within. An enlightened person is one whose whole being is illuminated by the light of inner truth. Truth is identical with the divine force, pure consciousness, or almighty God. In the light of that truth, great souls unveil the mystery of creation.

The potential for attaining enlightenment exists in every human being. A partial manifestation of intuitive knowledge can be observed in our day-to-day life. Through the power of intuition, talented poets and artists perceive extraordinary beauty. Through that power, scientists develop new formulas. Without relying on logic, people sometimes attain higher knowledge. With the dawning of intuitive power, the force of reason fades away. Some unfold and expand the flow of intuition with the help of spiritual practices, whereas in others, intuition remains dormant. Unless that power is awakened, the intellect cannot be fully purified. Only in the light of intuitive wisdom can one have a true picture of dharma.

Usually, we see this world in two different ways. First, we perceive objects through the senses and then the mind, ego, and intellect analyze them. Keen observation leads us to scientific exploration. The other way of knowing objects is through the heart. Gifted artists, poets, seers, saints, and sages experience truth directly through their hearts. They observe not only external objects, but their own mental modifications, attitudes, and tendencies. They are the knowers of the means as well as of the goal.

Without perfect knowledge, both the intellect and the heart are incomplete. The intellect is incomplete because it relies on reasoning. Usually the heart aspect of the human personality is not attuned to divine illumination. Without purification, one should not rely exclusively on either the intellect or the feelings of the heart. Ordinarily, one gains knowledge of a certain object through the intellect. Then one must test its validity in the light of not only logic, but of the intuition as well. The intellect is an inner instrument and, if defective, it can arrive at an incorrect conclusion. Information gained by the intellect must be verified. The function of the intellect, supported by intuition, can guarantee that knowledge is genuine. Such an illumined intellect cannot make a mistake at all. The intellect may be compared to mathematics, a means for understanding the truth through exact formulas. Intuitive knowledge, on the other hand, is like a fully awakened eye, which comprehends the totality of truth spontaneously.

With the dawning of intuitive knowledge, the veil of ignorance is removed forever. Such a fortunate aspirant, whose intuition is awakened, begins receiving inspiration and guidance from within. Without any effort on his part, he attains freedom from all doubts. He knows that his knowledge is self-evident and therefore does not need to be verified through reasoning. This is the highest state of knowledge. Compared to this, intellectual knowledge is certainly inferior. However, for a scientific study of the objective world, the intellect is the highest tool. While living in the world we discriminate right from wrong and good from bad through the intellect. All our decisions are made by the intellect. But a decision made with full confidence and clarity comes from the realm beyond the intellect. That which lies beyond the intellect is the divine force, where everything, whether manifest or unmanifest, is ever known. Knowledge of one's self-existence is attained not through the intellect but through that divine light within. No one ever needs to verify the knowledge of his self-existence.

The highest truth is hidden in itself, but its external form is reflected by the mirror of creation. That is how the inner truth manifests or evolves from absolute to immanent. Through the intellect, one may postulate the existence of

pleasant. He also resolves to achieve the good by employing only the right means. Such a person remains happy while performing his actions and remains happy when he achieves the results. Those who work hard without discrimination and proper understanding of the goals and means suffer from insecurity and fear. They are the ones who become influenced by the opinions and interpretations of narrow-minded, self-centered teachers. They also fail to understand the appropriateness of a given duty at a particular time and place. They may work hard, thinking they are performing right duties, but gain no positive result. From a practical standpoint, performing one's duties skillfully is more important than performing them selflessly. While the power of discrimination can help one understand how to perform one's duties skillfully, selflessness is a virtue of the heart. Only if there is a balance between these two in performing actions can one attain freedom from bondage. Lacking proper discrimination, people busy themselves in searching for pleasure from worldly objects. They also lack foresight, so the scope of their search remains confined to the moment. The vast future which is constantly slipping into the present is not taken into account.

By expanding one's worldview, sharpening one's intellect, and knowing the appropriateness of time and place in regard to one's personal and societal duties, one can become a perfect karma yogi. Such a karma yogi is master of his karmas and all their consequences. He tears apart the rope of karmic bondage with the powerful tool of karma itself. On the other hand, those with deluded intellect can perform their actions lovingly and selflessly, but still remain in the bondage of karma as they perform actions in an unskilled manner.

To reiterate, there should be a balance between religion and science, and between emotion and intellect, between personal duties and social welfare. Every aspect of life should be in perfect harmony. All activities, whether mental, verbal, or physical, should be guided by the light of inner truth. Humans cannot attain peace and happiness through intellectual discoveries alone. The power of the intellect and worldly resources should revolve around universal dharma, so that human beings can use them as a means for higher achievement. In our modern world, some people are convinced that truth is that which can be proved through empirical means. That is an extremely narrow definition. As scientists are involved in studying various facets of the truth in the external world, seekers should devote time to systematically exploring within themselves. There should be ongoing research in the inner world as well as the outer. We can make the best use of our empirical knowledge if we combine it with knowledge of inner reality. Science can offer means and comforts, whereas spirituality can help us employ them for higher achievement. With the help of science, we spend less time and energy to attain a comfortable life. If inspired spiritually, we can devote a significant part of our time and energy to our spiritual growth. Free from worldly worries, we can concentrate our minds and contemplate the higher truth. Science gives us mass production of objects and can help us meet the needs and necessities of all.

In the absence of spiritual harmony, as is the case today, our desires grow and we feel miserable. In spite of possessing more than we need, we remain dissatisfied and consequently work harder to achieve more. The tendency of possessiveness is the cause of dissatisfaction, worries, insecurity, and fear. It is beyond the capacity of science to help such people since nothing is enough for them. Spirituality alone can make them feel that they have enough and give them a sense of lasting satisfaction.

Before we try to bring science and spirituality together, we must become familiar with the fundamental principles of each. We have become familiar with science, but spirituality is still foreign to us. First, we should study its ethical aspect and integrate this with science. Spiritually-based morality can lead modern science in a constructive direction. In the next stage, we must practice the higher aspects of spirituality including the discipline of the body, mind, and senses. Science combined with that stage of spirituality becomes metaphysics; then there is no difference between science and spirituality. These two modes of knowledge, one related to the external world and the other to the inner world, together can help human beings attain perfection here and now.

Our system of education must incorporate the higher values of universal religion. If these are instilled, our children will transcend the limitations imposed by religion. They will study their own book of life, and unfold their inner potentials. They will not rely exclusively on the information they gain from others; they will become self-reliant. They will neither propagate narrow-minded dogmas nor oppose temples, mosques, or churches. Without disregarding their own traditional values, they will respect the common spiritual heritage of mankind.

Religious teachings that conflict with social duties create disharmony in personal and collective life. An exclusive emphasis on rituals and ceremonies does not allow human beings to explore the higher reality as explained by that particular religion. On the other hand, if a religion encourages only intellectualism and ignores the emotional aspects of humanity, it turns into mere philosophy. If it emphasizes only renunciation, it damages human growth in the material world. The dharma of mankind must have a balance between all these factors. For a happy and healthy life, and to attain enlightenment here and now, we must create a bridge between intellect and emotion. One must remain religious, but not fanatical. One should respect others without undermining oneself. One should work hard and share the fruits of one's actions with one's fellow beings. In a word, "Light thy own lamp and be a light to all."

Religion is supposed to remove weakness from the individual. Individuals constitute society. The problems of society can be worked out only by helping individuals become strong and self-reliant. Religion must include provisions to help the oppressed members of society. Religion must have equality as its major doctrine. We should not hesitate to discard a religion that inspires animosity, hatred, and jealousy in our hearts. A religion that helps us transcend our animal tendencies, that helps us become fully evolved human beings, and that helps us recognize the Divine within, is true religion.

CHAPTER FIVE

SELF-REALIZATION

HUMAN BIRTH IS NOT an accidental phenomenon. It has a purpose. A human being is born to accomplish a goal. As he grows, he gains coordination between his brain and sensory organs. Then coordination between his brain and mind arises. He begins thinking systematically, and his psychophysical activities become goal-oriented. Behind all his thoughts, speech, and actions, there is a purpose; in fact, it is his aim to find within himself that which leads a human being to think, speak, or act in the first place. Due to his incomplete knowledge, he fails to envision his goal in its totality and perfection. However, depending on the degree of his understanding, he sets up his goal and strives to achieve it through the means he thinks are most efficient.

As he moves along the stream of life, he learns from his experiences, gains knowledge, modifies his resolutions, and consequently expands the vision of his goal and ideals. This is an ongoing process. As a result of his thinking, the concepts of family, society, nation, culture, and civilization are born. He keeps refining his thinking process until he is fully convinced that he has comprehended the highest goal of life. He also uses the power of thought to invent the most suitable means and resources to accomplish his task. His view of his goal and the way in which he employs all available means and resources constitute his philosophy of life. All of humanity develops in this way. Those who study the nature of life come to realize the goal—a goal which presupposes the means and vice versa.

All human beings are born with the means and resources necessary to attain their goals, but must learn how to use their resources efficiently and skillfully. The power of thought is the highest tool through which one can decide what ought to be done and what ought to be avoided. The resolution to act and the process of action follow the direction of the power of thought. A human being tries to know the purpose of life and the means to achieve it. He wonders who he is, from where he has come, and ultimately where he will go. Through the power of thought, he also tries to know the very nature of his desires, thoughts, feelings, and innate tendencies. Thought does not allow him to rest until he has unveiled all the mysteries of life. The highest mystery that a human being wants to unveil is to know the nature of thought itself, the source from which the thinking process originates, and ultimately, he wants to learn the true nature of his own self. The stream of life may change its course; it may shift from one state to another; it may become manifest or unmanifest, but it never stops flowing. It moves on until it merges with the ocean, the pure supreme consciousness.

The selection of the right path is an important step toward achieving the goal. A human being should employ only the right means to follow the path. As he walks on the path, he gains experiences that help him understand the reliability of his approach. His first experience becomes the foundation for the next one, and thus, through a long chain of experiences, he builds the philosophy of his life. His philosophy and its constant application lead him to the goal. A human being should learn to compose himself and create a balance in all aspects of life. As long as a person lives in this world, he cannot function independently of his external or internal life. He has to grow both externally and internally. Growth in the external world means being a master over worldly objects, not a slave to them. He should be resourceful so that he can contemplate within, with a minimum of distractions from the external world. The purpose of life is to attain eternal bliss and become the lord of one's life, to know the vast unknown and rise above internal and external conflicts.

Nothing is more mysterious than life itself, and there is no peace without penetrating that mystery. The mystery lies deep in the stream of life. Eternal knowledge lies not in the outer world, but in the center of consciousness. Being identical to consciousness, every human being is endowed with that infinite knowledge. The only thing needed to know oneself is to withdraw one's mind from the external world and focus one's energy to explore the truth within. Along with the practice of meditation, one should also practice the proper method of contemplation. One should apply the power of thought, through which one will come to recognize that consciousness is the center of life. The life of all living beings depends on consciousness. One should learn to begin a dialogue with oneself. The study of genuine scriptures and the company of the wise can help one understand which means are appropriate to achieve the goal and which are not. Purity of the means and their proper application guarantee an auspicious ending. A human being should not become indifferent toward the means, lest his quest for self-realization remain a mere dream. He should not mistake dispassion, nonattachment, or indifference for dejection, hopelessness, or complacency. Courage, enthusiasm, and sincere effort are the driving forces to accomplish any given task. On the grounds of vigor, a positive attitude, and hope, a human being can successfully design the mansion of his future life. However, he should be careful to distinguish constructive and useful desires, ambitions, and curiosities from useless ones.

A human being is his own best friend and also his own worst enemy. He, himself, is the cause of his rise and fall. A human life is like a boat floating in the ocean of *samsara* (cycles of time), transmigrating worldly existence. Those who row their boat skillfully cross the ocean, whereas others drown again and again. There is no greater loss than letting the boat of life flounder uselessly.

One should not allow a pessimistic worldview to take over one's mind. Through a positive attitude toward life and life's circumstances, a human being can accomplish his goal. All the good and bad, constructive and destructive, divine and animal tendencies coexist in the human heart. Truthfulness, amity, compassion, generosity, and the desire for knowledge are higher qualities. By cultivating these qualities, a human being rises up and unfolds the divine within. On the other hand, hatred, jealousy, laziness, and negligence are qualities that force a human being to act like an animal. Through proper thinking and spiritual practice, he learns to replace his animal qualities with divine qualities. The more he nurtures his higher qualities, the more he grows in the spiritual realm. When all the lower qualities are replaced by divine qualities, a human being turns into a sage.

Through effort, a human being either achieves the goal or fails. While treading the path, he should not be discouraged by the possibility of failure. He must not allow hopelessness to come in his way. He should be confident of success. He should not undermine his inner strength nor doubt his capacity to achieve the goal. He should not forget the goal of life even for a single moment. If he remembers that his purpose is self-realization, hopelessness cannot arise. The desire for self-realization is a great force in itself.

A human being should learn to organize his worldly life so that the external world does not consume too much of his time and energy. By taking care of his duties lovingly and skillfully, a human being establishes harmony in his personal, family, and social life. A peaceful environment allows him to explore the higher reality, which is more important than the reality of the manifest world. A person running away from his duties and rightful obligations disturbs himself as well as others. No one attains freedom by running away from his duties. One should learn to perform one's duties with the help of right means. Right means are those which help one achieve one's goal, without hurting others and without disturbing their goals and duties. In order to perform one's duties through right means, one should sharpen one's intellect and stay in touch with the power of discrimination. Before committing oneself to the performance of duties, one should study the appropriateness of time and place. Any situation, circumstance, or worldly object can become a great tool for spiritual unfoldment provided an aspirant knows how to use them wisely and skillfully. Making the best use of all of life's situations, events, and circumstances is the art of successful living.

We should not become attached to the objects of the world. All that has come and is yet to come should be considered a gift from God. All pleasant and unpleasant situations should be taken positively. Nothing can happen in life unless there is a purpose set by a higher force. Every circumstance is offered from above as a means to achieve the goal. We waste a precious part of our lives thinking about objects that are not yet obtained. It is better to work constructively in the present than to worry about the future. Disregarding the importance of the present, people are preoccupied with memories of the past and anxiety about the future. We should remember that the past never comes back, and the future comes only in the form of the present. By making the best use of the resources available in the present, we can create a bright future.

The present is born from the womb of the past; similarly, the future rests in the womb of the present. It is not by becoming anxious about the future, but rather by awakening one's inner potentials here and now, that one can attain the goal of life. A human being is capable of creating his future as he wants it to be. By worrying about the past and the future, we gain nothing, but certainly entangle ourselves with the rope of attachment. A thought which cannot be brought into action is a source of dissipation of inner strength. We need to think not merely for the sake of thinking, but rather for the sake of attaining the goal through thoughtful action.

Action is the ground for the journey of life. Without performing actions, a human being cannot survive even for a moment. There are three inherent forces in nature: the powers of light, activity, and inertia. Through their functioning, nature never allows anyone or anything to be inactive. It is nature's law that no one can survive without performing actions. Once a human being performs an action, he inevitably obtains the result. Sometimes he receives the fruit of his action immediately in this very lifetime, sometimes in his next life. However, those who know the secret of performing their actions selflessly and skillfully are free from the fruits of their actions, and thus are free from the bondage of karma.

Under the guidance of the supreme divine force, nature carries on all its visible and invisible activities. Deluded by ignorance, human beings identify themselves as the "doers" of the actions and, as a result, bind themselves with the rope of actions. They forget that the whole universe has evolved from God and is pervaded by him. No one can really own the objects of the world. One can enjoy them, but cannot own them forever. One should not forget the purpose of having worldly objects, and certainly should not get attached to them while using them. A person forgets the highest goal of life, considers worldly objects to be his goal, and thus bondage begins. He constantly thinks of getting things, yet once they are at hand he suffers from the fear of losing them. All his activities in life are motivated by desire and attachment. A human being should learn to perform his actions in such a way that he is not bound to their fruits. This is possible if he constantly remembers the three following principles:

1. Renounce the fruits of all actions.

2. Consider yourself to be an instrument in the hands of the Divine instead of identifying yourself as a "doer."

3. Consider rightful actions to be your duty and perform them only for the sake of duty.

A human being should not become indifferent to his duties and responsibilities. According to the Bhagavad Gita, he should know what is right action and what is wrong action, and should perform only those actions that are right. He should never become inactive. However, his activities must not lead to his downfall. Although it is not always easy to comprehend which actions are right, which are wrong, and which are neutral, he can safely approach the performance of karma by taking refuge in the scriptures and in the examples set by the wise. He should try his best to perform only those actions which seem to be right at that time and place. A human being should not identify himself as a "doer" and should surrender the fruits of his actions to the Divine.

By performing actions, an aspirant attains freedom from bondage, provided he surrenders the fruits of his actions to the supreme truth. The difference between an ordinary person and an enlightened person is that the former performs his actions out of desire and attachment, whereas the latter performs the same actions just for the sake of duty. At the same time, the aspirant should not mistake complacency and inertia for desirelessness. It is important to fix a goal before he begins performing an action. Without a concrete goal, a person will not put his whole heart into the action. His lack of sincerity and wholeheartedness will prevent him from reaching the goal. Desirelessness springing from laziness, inertia, and complacency is as bad as desire and attachment. He who thinks about his duties but does not perform them becomes a victim of laziness, attachment, and fear. These are the greatest enemies to be subdued in life.

Performing actions only for the sake of enjoying their fruits is a source of bondage. Performing actions without desiring the fruit is a great path to attain freedom from bondage, but it is difficult to perform actions without a goal. Human beings do not find an incentive to do something if they have nothing to gain. The best way is to set up a goal, work hard, perform the necessary actions, reach the goal, and immediately surrender the fruits to the almighty supreme Lord.

An aspirant begins his spiritual life with the performance of selfless actions. Through selfless service he purifies his mind and heart, and he attains freedom from his normal duties and obligations. By performing actions he gathers means, overcomes his inner conflicts, gains blessings from those whom he serves, and gradually, being free from external disturbances, he channels his energies toward self-realization. Such a karma yogi, the performer of selfless actions, attains peace even before he has a direct experience of the omniscient truth. Free from anxiety, he performs his actions selflessly and lovingly. He is at peace while performing his actions, and eternal joy is his after he concludes the drama of life. While performing his duties, he remains free from the stain of actions. While living in the world, he remains above it. The principle of selfless action is the essence of the path of action, the path of knowledge, the path of love, and the path of renunciation.

By using his discrimination, a person can change his circumstances to be more in his favor. He can also have a spontaneous feeling of which actions are right and which are not. His discrimination reminds him of the importance of the present moment. A person busy in making the best use of the present automatically remains unaffected by memories of the past and anxiety about the future. An aspirant should not waste a single moment of his life, for no one can predict what will happen tomorrow.

Every individual has the power of discrimination. He is also fully equipped with all the means he needs to accomplish his task, but in spite of these gifts he still suffers. There is no greater loss than not being aware of one's resources. He has the powers of thought and discrimination. He has the power of will to execute his actions. He has resources, but because of negligence he fails to reach the goal of life. A human being knows that he is not moving toward the goal. He knows he is not making an effort, and he also knows that living such a life is painful. Nevertheless, out of ignorance he does not allow himself to move from the spot where he has been sitting for ages. Instead of searching for the truth, he is content with his fear of hell or desire to go to heaven. He knows that his longing for peace and happiness is more meaningful than the suggestions given by religious teachers. Yet he listens to them more than he listens to his own inner voice. A human being knows that the journey cannot be completed unless he, himself, walks the path. Still, he believes in the empty promises of preachers. Human beings have formed a habit of blaming God, the devil, ghosts, and spirits for their unhappiness. The journey to peace and happiness can begin only after recognizing one's inner potentials. An aspirant should gain confidence, cultivate his inner strength, become determined to dispel his fear and insecurity. He should commit himself to spiritual practices and unfold the infinite power within. After getting in touch with his *Atma-Shakti,* the power of Atman, he will realize his oneness with God or pure consciousness.

Once an aspirant is inspired to know the highest truth, he cannot waste time; every breath of life will be filled with inspiration. The experience of emptiness that once made him feel dejected, frustrated, and dissatisfied becomes the stimulus for a constructive new way of being. He stops wasting his time, and gets ready to find perfection. He turns his face from the objects he used to love and preserve. He reevaluates his relationships and his interaction with worldly objects. In the light of discrimination, he comprehends the true nature of his friends, relatives, family, and worldly objects. He cares for them, but not at the cost of his inner peace. In the light of discrimination, he attains freedom from the defects of his lower mind.

The more the aspirant moves inward, the more he finds the necessary resources coming together. After overcoming poverty from within, he becomes a master of his external world. Every aspect of his life is illuminated with the light of inner awareness. Once this inner journey begins, and once he starts getting glimpses of his eternal kingdom, he never becomes distracted by the charms and temptations of the world. Because of the powers of discrimination, will, and determination, and ultimately the grace of the supreme divine force, he realizes that he is fully equipped with all the necessary means and resources. He knows that there is no reason to be insecure. There is no reason to doubt his success. In such an aspirant's life, there is no place for hopelessness.

In the initial stages of the spiritual journey, the intellect seems to be the highest faculty of thinking, knowing, and discriminating. As we dive within, we realize that the intellect is simply an inner instrument. However, it is the finest instrument through which the power of discrimination flows. The intellect is an evolute of primordial nature. The power of discrimination which resides in the intellect is illumination from the divine force. The divine force is higher than the intellect and primordial nature. As all the objects of the world are illuminated with the light of the sun, similarly the intellect, mind, and senses receive their illumination from the inner light of the divine force. In order to attain spiritual wisdom, an aspirant should purify, sharpen, and train the intellect so that it functions under the guidance of that divine force. He should not allow his ego to come forward and convince him that he, as a body-mind organism, is the highest truth. Egoism is the most subtle pollutant of all and the most difficult to eliminate.

There are two ways to purify one's mind, ego, and intellect. In the light of divine illumination, an aspirant's whole being is transformed. His senses, mind, and intellect are purified; all the mental vasanas, the subtle impressions of the past, are washed off. At the dawn of enlightenment, that kind of purification takes place spontaneously. However, one should not wait for it passively. When the time is ripe, when an aspirant is ready, and the preliminaries have been completed, the grace of the Divine descends and the seeker is blessed with inner illumination. An aspirant's duty is to make a sincere effort to purify his thoughts, speech, and actions. With the practice of *asanas*, yogic exercises, he purifies his body. With the help of *pranayama*, breathing exercises, he purifies his nadis, the energy channels and pranic vehicles. Through pranayama, he destroys the veil that obstructs the light. With the help of meditation he removes the impurities of the mind, and as a result obtains a clear vision of the divine light within.

When a human being is not aware of the existence of the Divine, and therefore considers his sensory knowledge to be the sole reality, he moves away from the truth. In our modern world, there is an enormous emphasis on developing sensory perceptions and gaining experiences. The main purpose of our modern system of education is to teach children how to use their senses to gain knowledge of the objects of the world. There is no end to such knowledge since objects are many and the power of the senses is limited. The same is true with the peace and happiness that we expect to attain through the senses. Sensory pleasures can never make us permanently happy. We must not mistake sensory perception for the perfect truth. By clinging to the knowledge received through the senses, one creates the basis for attachment and aversion. Out of attachment, a person's mind is pulled toward the things he desires. He stores the subtle impression of every one of his sensory experiences in his unconscious mind, and they in turn fuel his desires. Once that vicious cycle starts, a human being is completely lost.

The only way to get out of that cycle is to accept the superiority of discrimination, willpower, and divine inspiration over sensory perceptions and cognition. An aspirant must change his worldview and start looking at life from a higher perspective. He should break this cycle systematically, step by step. First, he should look at the nature of the transitory objects and the amount of satisfaction derived from them. Through honest analysis, he realizes that the objects of the senses are a source of joy as long as they are not in hand. Once they are attained, the senses and mind become dissatisfied and search for other objects. This knowledge helps the seeker change his perception. A feeling of dispassion arises in his heart. That knowledge-born dispassion inspires him to change the course of his life and begin exploring the possibility of finding eternal peace and happiness. The seeker's spiritual desire consumes all his trivial cravings and attachments. His power of discrimination becomes active. He purifies his thoughts, speech, and actions, and as a result of that purity, one day he receives divine illumination from above.

One should not be preoccupied with pleasure and pain all the time. These experiences are common to all species. There is no pleasure without pain. These are twin laws of nature and the purpose of human birth is to transcend these laws. The highest good lies not in running after pleasure and fighting against pain, but in rising above both and attaining the state that is eternal and perfect. One should remember the transitory nature of worldly objects and the pain and pleasure derived from them. One should also remember that external phenomena follow the directions of the inner force. Everything taking place in the external world is a mere reflection of one's inner states. Working with one's inner states is more important than getting involved in pleasant or unpleasant experiences. A person with a composed mind can utilize all circumstances, whether they are pleasant or unpleasant. A spiritually awakened person makes the best use of unpleasant circumstances because he treats them with dispassion and indifference. He spends pleasant days expressing love, compassion, and generosity toward others. A person endowed with the power of discrimination remains unperturbed in all phases of life. He knows that both pleasure and pain are equally disturbing experiences. How balanced a person is during turmoil indicates how evolved he is. The closer a person is to the Divine, the less he is affected by pleasure and pain.

Love, compassion, generosity, and humility are great virtues. Human beings endowed with these virtues are naturally inclined toward high thinking and simple living. They are the ones who make the best use of their happy days. Because of their humility, they are free from egotism. Such a person remains happy even during difficult periods in life. On the other hand, those who consider the objects of the senses to be the only source of happiness remain dissatisfied since there is no end to desires, while objects are limited. Achieving worldly pleasures feeds their egos, which in turn overshadows the higher virtues. In spite of experiencing many pleasures, such people remain miserable.

It is crucial to cultivate love, compassion, and generosity so that one can transcend self-centered awareness. A generous person constantly thinks of others' welfare. Selfless service becomes a central part of his life, which helps him awaken all of the other virtues. Rather than emphasizing his personal benefit, he gives priority to the welfare of the whole society. A person driven by the force of generosity and selfless service crosses the boundaries of self-centered "I" and "my" awareness and realizes himself to be a part of all humanity. Only then does he truly comprehend the pains and miseries of others. He finds great joy in sharing their suffering. The more he serves and the more he gives, the more he purifies his mind and heart. As a result of his inner purity, there springs forth a stream of compassion which wipes out the remaining less noticeable traces of selfishness. With the removal of selfishness, he naturally attains freedom from desires, attachment, and egotism. A real desire to know the truth arises. The desire for truth or enlightenment is the most auspicious phenomenon in spiritual life. Such a desire leads one on the path of truth. One worships none but the truth. One cares for none but the truth. One directs one's energies only toward the truth.

The way in which a person thinks is the way he forms his personality and designs his destiny. The way he thinks determines the quality of the fruits derived from his actions.

By thinking one-pointedly, the mind becomes absorbed in the object one is thinking about. Such thinking is termed contemplation. Through contemplating on almighty, compassionate God, one's mind and heart are filled with divine love. By thinking of the welfare of all creatures, one attains the greatest gift, unconditional love for all. Pure love by its very nature brings the lover and the beloved together, for in pure love, a sense of duality between the lover and the object of love cannot exist. As long as there are karmic impurities in the heart, a person remains selfish. His selfishness does not allow him to experience the oneness between himself and the object he loves. In the absence of selfishness and karmic impurities from the past, a human being is free from all afflictions. Selfishness and subtle traces of the past are the foundation of all pain and misery. One can attain freedom from selfishness by living in the company of the wise and serving others without any expectations. Karmic impurities and subtle traces of previous deeds can be washed off by cultivating dispassion within. One should look at the inevitable consequences of unwholesome actions and resolve not to commit the same actions again and again. By not doing unwholesome actions, an aspirant stops sowing unhealthy new karmic seeds. By performing right actions, he sows the seeds of virtues.

A human being becomes the slave of his ego when he thinks of selfish gains. A selfish person dwells in a state of doubt since his conscience constantly reminds him of his wrong attitude. On the one hand, he is pulled by his selfish desires, and on the other, he is alarmed by his inner voice. He's torn apart by these two forces. But he who listens to the voice of his inner soul and performs his actions under the guidance of his discrimination rises above his egocentric awareness. He is the one who attains foresight, and thereby the power of discrimination guides him on the path of righteousness. A human being who lacks the power of discrimination performs his actions without being aware of their consequences. Most of the time, he is driven by his desires, whims, and primitive urges. He usually does not know what the truth is, and even if he knows, he fails to practice it in his thoughts, speech, and actions.

The power of discrimination is the greatest of all the benevolent forces within. With the help of contemplation and meditation, an aspirant should unfold this power and learn to distinguish right actions from unwholesome ones. He should execute his power of discrimination to analyze his own inner states so that he can be aware of his strengths and weaknesses. However, the recognition of these strengths and weaknesses should not be allowed to feed his ego or lead him toward self-condemnation. The purpose of this inner analysis is to unfold the good qualities and remove the unhelpful ones. The more an aspirant hides his weaknesses, the more they grow. One should acknowledge one's weak points and resolve to remove them once and for all.

Even at a collective level, acknowledgment of the weak points of society and a resolution to remove them is extremely important. History reminds us that a particular society, community, or nation retards its growth when, out of rigidity or omission, it does not acknowledge its weaknesses. Fearing humiliation or suffering from inferiority complexes, such a society justifies its weakness by pretending it is a great quality. Such a society or community moves toward its own doom. A human being or a society purifies itself, not by hiding its defects and weaknesses, but by removing them. For human mistakes and weaknesses, religions have offered a system of penances, but according to the Upanishads, there is no better penance than the resolution not to repeat the same mistake.

Repentance is the first step toward the correction of one's mistake. It helps one to acknowledge the mistake and to convince the mind that it is not good to commit such mistakes over and over again. The second step is to confess the weakness in front of those who are loving, considerate, and compassionate. By taking this second step, a human being attains freedom from his guilt, fears, and self-condemnation, and thereby restores his power of will. He attains freedom from his own mood of dejection and reestablishes his cheerfulness. The third step is to recall his power of determination, resolve to withdraw his mind from such mistakes, and commit himself to positive actions. Psychology calls this reeducation, whereas in the language of spirituality it is called self-transformation.

A person walking the path of self-transformation should be aware of his egoism. Even after practicing the great virtues of truthfulness, nonviolence, and so on, a person can feed his ego. The ego related to the realm of spirituality is more subtle and injurious than the ego arising out of one's worldly success. By practicing diligently, one may attain concentration of the mind, one may speak the truth, and one may serve others, but one cannot realize the truth unless one surrenders one's ego to the higher self. A human being may be very close to his goal, but because of the wall of egoism between him and the goal, he remains alien to his own inner kingdom. After rising above his egocentric awareness, he finds that not only is he within the universe but the universe is within him. It is only then that he loves all and excludes none. One who does not love his fellow beings cannot love God at all.

A human being is miserable if he fails to unfold and use his inner potentials. He is weak, and therefore cannot help or serve others regardless of his desire to do so. In order to unfold his inner potentials, he must purify his ego or surrender it to the higher reality. After renouncing slavery to his ego, he emerges from the confines of his body, senses, and mind. Through the uninterrupted practice of meditation and contemplation, the seeker one day attains illumination through discrimination. Illumined with the light of discrimination, he enters the kingdom of his eternal heart. He finds his whole life driven by the power of discrimination and faith, and performs his actions under their guidance. Unless these two principles—discrimination and faith—are fully unfolded, a human being cannot rise above the spheres of the lower mind and ego. He cannot spontaneously distinguish the right course of action, and he cannot perform his actions wholeheartedly. Without perfect faith in the higher reality, he cannot attain freedom from his own anxiety and insecurity. Without discrimination and faith, he lives in a state of doubt. Therefore, the most important step toward self-transformation is to shed one's ego, surrender it to the higher reality, and thereby attain the light of discrimination and pure faith. Once this step is completed, there will not be any conflict in one's thoughts, speech, and actions.

Humanity is suffering from its ego-born differences and inequality. Today, people discriminate against their own brothers and sisters simply on the basis of race, religion, caste, or complexion. In order to be free from these problems, a political settlement alone is not enough. When all human beings understand that their suffering has been brought on by ego, they will resolve their differences. They will throw aside the confinements of race, caste, religion, and sectarian feelings. Instead of identifying with a particular group or community, they will identify themselves as human beings. Then they will love everyone else as if they were their own family members. They will find joy in renouncing their rights for the welfare of others. They will respect the feelings and rights of others more than their own. They will quickly resolve their external and internal conflicts.

Floating in the eternal stream of life, a human being has gone through countless life states. In his perennial journey, he has assumed numerous forms and names. He came and went while passing through the gates of death and birth and gained the experience of various species. No one knows how long it has taken to be born in a human body, wherein one receives the powers of will, discrimination, thought, and so on. The stream of life is filled with experiences of, and reactions to, all his births and deaths. Death and birth seem to be an unending cycle. After a human being is born, he goes to the lap of death, and from death, he comes to the lap of birth. That process continues until he attains knowledge and realizes his true identity with the supreme truth. Through the power of discrimination, he distinguishes himself from the nonself and thereby disidentifies himself from pains and miseries. A human being should be grateful to the One who has given him the power of discrimination. The self-shining, supreme truth is the center of his consciousness. The intellect receives its discriminatory ability from the very center of consciousness. By making the best use of one's discrimination, one attains a state of fearlessness.

A human being can purify his mind and heart only after he has organized his external life properly. A mind scattered in the external world does not have time to contemplate the purpose of life. A heart distracted by conflicting emotions cannot have room for selfless love, compassion, and service.

A human being should learn to adjust himself to his family, society, and community in such a way that he can create a peaceful environment for himself and others. All the social, moral, and ethical laws are meant to establish and maintain peace and harmony in society. A human being can attain his personal goal, without getting in the way of the welfare of others, if he keeps love as his central focus. By loving all, he practices other great principles such as nonviolence, truthfulness, nonpossessiveness, contentment, and so on. Love and negativity cannot coexist. Love for all human beings purifies one's heart. As a result, one's consciousness expands. One redefines one's conception of love, and instead of loving human beings alone, all of creation falls within the range of one's love. The thread of love unites all the diversities into one nondual, unitary consciousness. By loving all, one loves the universal soul, God. As supreme love unfolds, conflicts, differences, hatred, jealousy, and selfishness disappear once and for all. One who loves all, considering this universe to be a manifestation of the supreme divine force, attains knowledge of the nondual, absolute reality. He realizes this universe as his own elaboration.

Human beings can attain the summum bonum of life if they have a sound foundation in their family institution and society. They cannot avoid the impact of their family or the community environment in which they are born and raised. One's environment is created by all the members of family and society. It requires collective effort and general awareness to restructure family and social values and bring a qualitative change conducive to human growth.

Nonstealing and nonpossessiveness are the two great virtues that help us maintain a peaceful environment in both family and society. Human beings should learn to respect others' thoughts and feelings. They should be more sensitive to the rights of others than to their own. People should strive to maintain the rights of their children, brothers, sisters, spouse, friends, and neighbors. They should be able to analyze their own rights and never trespass against the rights of others. A healthy society does not need to be guarded by police. Law and order should be accepted and maintained willingly, lovingly, and with full understanding. A healthy society does not need commandments, since it knows the value of commitment for its own sake. The people of such an evolved society care for and help one another. They have the courage to make others happy at the cost of their personal pleasures. They are the ones who enjoy the path of selfless service. Everyone receives the benefit of others' generosity, love, compassion, and wisdom. Members of that evolved society attain the goal of life without facing too many distractions and disturbances. They find freedom and enlightenment as their birthright. Just by being born and raised in such a society, they are free from fear and insecurity. Unless we have such an evolved society, and unless we have an enlightening family environment, there is no hope for collective happiness.

Personal happiness can be attained, but only after prolonged and strenuous effort. Without a proper environment and healthy family institution, a person seeking self-enlightenment is forced to follow the path of renunciation. Out of thousands, just a few are inspired to attain the goal in seclusion. Many of the inspired ones drop their quest in the middle, and thus very few reach the goal. By improving the level of our awareness, and by creating a loving, generous, and understanding environment, we can enjoy all the objects of the world and still attain the highest goal of life. There is no need to seclude ourselves from our brothers and sisters, who love and care for us, and whom we love and care for. The process can begin by replacing our selfishness with love and selfless service.

We must not create a wall between our worldly and spiritual lives. People disorganized in their worldly life search for spiritual wisdom in seclusion; whereas, if organized properly, they can have all the means and resources that are of utmost importance for spiritual enlightenment. The purpose of having human life is to make the best use of the resources nature or God has given us. There are typically two kinds of people. Some are involved in the world and are busy with self-centered activities. Others renounce their families and do not participate in worldly life at all. People belonging to these two categories have an incomplete worldview, and therefore strive for their limited personal goals. There are very few people who use discrimination, work hard for their self-fulfillment, and at the same time contribute to the welfare of society.

In our modern age, where the standard of living has been facilitated by science and technology, we must learn to make the best use of our ample resources. A lifestyle that is suitable for both worldly fulfillment and spiritual enlightenment is the best. Those who strive to attain personal enlightenment and help others light their lamps are the true leaders of the human race. Blessed are those who are useful for themselves as well as others. They attain the highest goal of life here and now. Right in this mortal world they become immortal, and their wisdom guides humanity on the path of immortality.

Today's society is waiting for selfless, spiritually enlightened, well-balanced leaders to guide them in how to live happily here and hereafter. Such leaders or reformers will not come from outside our society. They have to be born, raised, and trained right in our own society. We must become our own guides, our own leaders, and we must enlighten our own lives. Get up, my friends, arise! Attain knowledge, and dedicate your lives to the service of your fellow beings.

CHAPTER SIX

HUMANISM

CONSIDERING OUR PRESENT circumstances, it seems that man-made, narrow "isms" cannot help us anymore. A religion that cannot coexist with modern science and technology is inadequate. Fortunately, people have begun exploring the possibility of a religion that can be practiced without conflicts and contradictions. Today, humanity is waiting for a religion that can be practiced any place and any time. The practices of existing religions have been confined to monasteries, temples, churches, and mosques. People have begun to question the usefulness of religions that are practiced only in designated places. It doesn't make sense for religious practices to be separated from everyday life. Religion has confined its practices and services to occasional ceremonies and festivals, and has even offered them to the public as a means of entertainment. Dissatisfied with such religious practices, human beings today are waiting for a religion that will be a part of their daily lives.

The Upanishads are the way to understand our religion and remodel it. Study of the Upanishads can help us structure a religion for all mankind. Through the study of the Upanishads, we can grasp the importance and inner significance of worship, ritual performances, and adoration of a personal God. The same Upanishads can open our eyes and help us transcend our limited concept of God. We can worship an image of God with a much greater philosophical and spiritual understanding, and as our knowledge grows and perspectives change, the worship of God through a symbol or image can be left behind. Consequently, we can aspire to realize God, and experience him within rather than worshiping him through a symbol or image.

The great philosophers, thinkers, and religious leaders across the centuries have repeatedly reformed religions. Their reformations and reinterpretations of religions were meant for all of mankind. They were followers of the original truth. Their message was for the whole world. In order to establish higher values in our religion we have to think through the minds of those sages. Peace and happiness are the prime concerns of religion, yet they cannot be obtained by adhering to the kind of Hinduism, Vaisnaivism, Shaivism, Jainism, Buddhism, Christianity, or Islam existing today. We need a religion that can help us understand that we are more than Hindus, Vaisnavites, Shaivites, Muslims, Christians, Buddhists, or Jainas. Free from our ethnocentric veils, we must recognize ourselves as human beings striving to become fully evolved. In order to understand and practice such a religion, we have to attain freedom from inequality and ignorance. People need to be educated. We have to transcend our racial vanity, and we have to search for a lifestyle to restructure a new, reformed society.

In order to bring peace and harmony to our society, we must look at our lives from a higher perspective. The more we understand the realities of life, the more we transcend the limitations of racial vanity, communal identities, and affiliation with a particular religion. When we rise above these limitations, our consciousness expands. We become part of the universe and the universe becomes part of us. The saints and sages of ancient India never propagated any particular faith or creed; they always presented the true nature of dharma, the eternal law that was helpful for all human beings alike. They had provisions for modifying their teachings so that they would be applicable to everyone living at various times and places. They consistently discouraged rigidity. Later, preachers imposed narrow-mindedness on the great teachings of the enlightened saints. Evidently, this was done for their selfish gain. Today, all of us are witnessing the exploitation of religion all over the world.

Over the last few centuries, people have introduced many new cults, sects, and creeds. They flourish for a few years and then disappear, leaving their stains on the pages of history. Like waves on the surface of the ocean, such religious paths come and go. They never endure, since they have selfishness as their foundation. In modern times, many religious beliefs are born every day in different parts of the world. They attract a core of people, build a following, accomplish their purpose, and soon disappear. Most of these religions are centered around a person. It is an important task for seekers to distinguish true dharma from these rigid sects, and practice the higher forms of truth that can unite us without hurting anyone. We must accept only that dharma which helps us foster the best and the highest in ourselves. We need a dharma which can stand by us all of the time, reminding us of our essential connection with the rest of humanity. We need a dharma which emphasizes practice more than theory. The more commandments, the more confusion. People surrender themselves to commandments under pressure of fear and guilt. Such commandments can momentarily suppress primitive tendencies, but they can never help us transform our personalities. Instead of grand exhortations, we need simple and practical guidelines that help us organize our lives.

The scriptures are full of gems of knowledge, but humanity for the most part is not aware of that treasure. Those who claim to be the leaders of society and custodians of its religions should study the actual needs of contemporary society. It is the responsibility of such preachers and leaders to present the wisdom of the scriptures in as simple a manner as possible. Their presentation should be understandable and beneficial to all. They should remember that when a person is suffering from sickness, he needs treatment, not lectures describing the nature of the disease. Today, humanity needs moral and intellectual revitalization.

Many of the ideals which were wonderful in ancient times are not applicable anymore. In ancient India, people lived in the lap of nature and did not need many worldly objects for a happy life. In those days, they studied and shared their knowledge while living in the forest. Today, rural civilization has been replaced by urban settlements. In this setting, people cannot live without considerable resources. We have strayed so far now that it is extremely difficult to go back to nature. The whole world is looking for balance and harmony in society. That balance can be found by bringing together the two great forces of spirituality and science. Present-day problems can be solved by creating harmony between realism and idealism.

Neither indifference toward worldly objects nor a materialistic attitude can bring peace and happiness to our lives. Indifference toward worldly objects makes people inactive, and that invites failure and dissatisfaction in life. Being indifferent, we also fail to make the best use of what we already have. While living in the world we must play our roles effectively, become resourceful and enjoy every moment of our lives. However, we must not forget the highest goal of life. We should learn to use the objects of the world as means to attain the highest goal. It is impossible to attain the goal without proper means.

In ancient times, material achievements were considered to be less important than spiritual achievements. Later, people excessively emphasized the spiritual outlook and undervalued worldly achievements. They forgot that great ideals can be nourished through worldly means. One cannot continue one's spiritual practices without organizing one's life in the external world; however, without having a foundation in spirituality, material growth also loses its luster. All the developing countries, including India, must work hard to gain material resources. On the other hand, the materially developed countries of the West should channel their resources toward helping individuals experience eternal peace.

There was once a great emphasis on achieving individual freedom. People strived to attain peace and happiness for themselves. Today, we cannot live in seclusion and cannot separate ourselves from the problems and concerns of the rest of society. How is it possible to disregard the problems of our neighbors? There is no way to be happy if our fellow beings are suffering from disease and poverty. Our communication media have brought us all together; we quickly hear and see each other's problems. To have concern for others is to be human. By being selfish and self-centered, we fall from our true human status. Now we must strive for peace and happiness as a group. Before committing ourselves to work together, we have to create a sense of equality. We have to raise our moral status and design a new world that is free from complexes and inequities.

In this age of high technology, no community or race can maintain its existence without associating with other communities and races. So there must be better understanding among human beings. We have to share one another's losses and gains. We have to learn from each other's experiences for our own growth and promote the growth of others. Rising above superiority and inferiority complexes, different groups of people must work together toward a common goal—that of peace and happiness. Different nations, religions, and cultures of the world must recognize their strengths and weaknesses.

The contribution of science and technology cannot be underestimated. Science has made the world quite small. Physical distances do not separate people the way they once did. Although people have begun sharing each other's material products, they do not share their thoughts and feelings. It appears that because material objects have brought them together, people have begun to regard each other as a means for gaining material benefits. Because of a lack of spiritual awareness, people consider this world to be the sole reality. Consequently, they are busy in the race for material development. Their materialistic worldview feeds their egos and creates inequality, discrimination, and odd complexes in our society.

The human race is suffering from ego-born narrow-mindedness. Discrimination exists, based on religion, color, and nationality. In the same locality, people are being discriminated against just because they are European or Asian, black or white, Hindu or Muslim. As long as these man-made divisions exist in our society, there is no hope for peace and happiness. We must understand that we are born as humans and all other identifications are superimposed on us later. Loving others and receiving love from others is our birthright. True freedom means loving all and hating none, including all and excluding none. In order to cultivate our humanity, we have to reach out to the hearts of our fellow beings. Political treaties and alliances are of little value unless there is a desire in every heart to overcome mutual differences which have been artificially imposed by selfish political, social, and religious leaders.

Removing differences and moving from diversity to unity are the essence of real spiritual practices. This process has to occur at every level of our individual and social lives. By realizing one reality within all, we will be able to purify our hearts and minds. This purification can lead us to the experience of the divine light within. Once we experience this inner truth, we will find ourselves to be a part of the universe, and the universe a part of us. Upon such realization here and now, we will not need to imagine a heaven apart from this universe. By loving all and excluding none, by sharing everything and possessing nothing, we will attain freedom from the fear of hell and the desire for heaven. We can have our own heaven here on earth.

Our interpersonal relationships must be based on the philosophy of universal brotherhood. The power of science and technology must be guided by the higher principles of ethics, morality, and spirituality. Science and religion, technological discoveries and spiritual wisdom, have to come together. Today there is no balance between science and spirituality, and as a result, science seems to be moving toward self-destruction. Instead of bringing peace, science has been creating fear.

With the help of science, humanity has reached the nuclear age. Scientific discoveries have brought a great change in our standard of living. As far as physical comforts based on material objects are concerned, we are far better off than our ancestors, but peace of mind has declined many times more than comforts and luxuries in the external world have increased. No matter how many things we invent with the help of intellectual knowledge, we cannot free ourselves from inequality, fear, and doubt. True freedom comes from within. In order to find that freedom, we have to withdraw our attention from the external world and make our minds inward. The solution to human problems can be found in the inner chamber of one's own heart. Unless one realizes the Divine, there is no way for a human being to attain eternal peace. The mind and intellect are the finest tools for knowing the objects of the world or exploring the truth within. However, they need to be trained so that they can discriminate right from wrong, and the good from the pleasant.

We should also be aware of the limitations of the mind and intellect. The intellect can lead us to the realization of the external world. It can come up with wonderful scientific discoveries, but it cannot fathom the absolute truth. It cannot guide us beyond the domain of the material world since it does not have a light of its own. The intellect functions under the guidance of a conscious force, Atman. The knowledge of Atman alone can reveal the totality and perfection of the truth. Illumined by the light of Atman, the intellect can change its course and begin comprehending the higher truth lying behind matter and material energies. Illumined by the knowledge of Atman, the intellect can comprehend the principle of universal brotherhood. Such an intellect can practice and enjoy *samatva* yoga, the yoga of equality or harmony.

Training of the intellect begins with the transformation of our attitude toward life and material goods. The mind should not be focused on running after worldly objects. We must employ our inner faculties to contemplate within. However, we must be aware of the fact that the mind and intellect are not the greatest forces. They receive their inspiration from the higher force of Atman. The intellect must carry on its duties of thinking, contemplating and analyzing the multileveled manifest world. But rather than becoming a victim of the ego, it must surrender itself to the divine force within. Such an intellect can help us become successful in the world, and at the same time, analyze our true nature within. In Indian philosophy, the intellect is described as a mirror that reflects the true nature of Atman. As long as that mirror is clean, the reflection is accurate. But when the mirror of the intellect is clouded with thought constructs, it presents a distorted reality. Purification, concentration, and an inward-turning of the intellect are necessary if we are to attain eternal peace and happiness.

People of today's age of high technology certainly have more material objects than the people of a century ago, but they seem to be more dissatisfied and frustrated than their forefathers. They seem to be more manipulative, possessive, and self-centered. The richer and more resourceful a person is, the more he exploits the oppressed members of society. He has an unending desire for "more," and he does not hesitate to fulfill his desires at the cost of others' welfare. Such an attitude cannot be cured by science. Without spiritual awareness, it is not possible to make the best use of scientific discoveries. By sharpening our intellects and training them for scientific discoveries, we bring more chaos to life. Purification and transformation is more important than sharpening the intellect for external achievements. A purified intellect can give one a better perspective of life. It can guide human destiny in the right direction. Purification of the intellect is not possible through the intellect itself. The intellect is clouded with the information it receives through sense perception. Such an intellect cannot rise above the limitations of time and space. It is the light of divine illumination that can guide the intellect beyond the realm of the senses and the material world.

People are still experimenting with the objects of the world. This experiment seems to be an unending process. So far humanity has not set up a definitive lifestyle to create happiness. Many people in the past have experienced the higher reality and have concluded that happiness lies within, not in the material world. However, their experience has not become the experience of all. Out of many, only a few follow the footsteps of the enlightened sages. They are the ones who attain happiness. They live in the world yet remain above it. Without inner illumination, external life cannot be made pure and ideal. External life must be illuminated by the divine light within. Freedom from pain and misery can be achieved by unveiling the secret of inner life. Once this is unveiled, we receive the divine message. The moment the veil is lifted and the ego is attuned to the higher self, our thoughts, speech, and actions follow the will of the Divine. Once there is balance between divine will and our worldly activities, we enjoy freedom here and now. One who has free access to the world within and without becomes a citizen of both worlds. He attains freedom, and eternal peace is his.

People want to live happy and peaceful lives, but in the absence of right means, their desires remain unfulfilled. Humanity is constantly striving to attain freedom from pain and misery. Many of the philosophers and thinkers in the past realized that human beings have infinite potential within, and that if they really want to achieve the state of freedom, it is possible for them to do so. Accomplished masters of yoga realized the power of will and with the help of that power attained the highest goal of life. If one person can attain freedom, why can't others? Every human being is equally equipped with all potentials and resources. If one human being can become a yogi and attain enlightenment, then certainly others can do the same. People are not born again and again for the sake of mere birth and death. Perfection is the goal they are trying to attain through their perennial journey of life. Human life is an opportunity. In this state, one has freedom either to move upward or downward. One can cast off one's limitations, expand one's awareness, and become divine. On the other hand, out of laziness and inertia, one may slip to lower states of existence. There cannot be a greater loss than missing the opportunity of human birth and having to start all over again.

Every person knows that the goal of his life is to attain peace and happiness. He also knows that others have the same purpose. All of humanity is working toward one objective: eternal joy. An individual is part of creation, and by excluding the whole, he cannot survive. However, out of ego, he acts as though he has separated himself from the totality of existence. This dichotomy persists only because of his ignorance. Considering oneself to be separate from the perfect, all-pervading universal truth is the main cause of all pain and misery. On the one hand, the ego draws a wall around itself, while on the other hand, the force of inner unity pulls the sense of individuality toward its inherent perpetual perfection. Even in nature, we can see this force in operation. Between individuals and creation, between external and internal phenomena, between manifest and unmanifest, there exists a force that always remains in perfect harmony and balance. That force inspires and sustains both parts of reality, the external and internal, the manifest and unmanifest. From the infinite existence of that force, this multifaceted universe receives sustenance. By drinking the nectar of that infinite divine force one attains immortality. In order to experience that immortal nectar, one has to penetrate the known and the unknown, the manifest and unmanifest. The path of yoga as described by the sages of the Upanishads is the way to penetrate the totality of the truth.

Long ago, personal enlightenment was considered to be the highest goal of life. In those days, it was the proper goal because people could accomplish their daily tasks with a minimum of support from others. Because there was no modern communication media, the news related to the problems of a person or a community did not spread very fast. Thus, people remained unaffected by the circumstances of others who lived at a distance. But with the advances in communication technology the situation has changed. Today's news about particular people or other cultures spreads rapidly. Furthermore, the present-day economy has made everyone interdependent. The affliction of any part of our society affects the entire human race. At this stage of our evolution we must think of the welfare of the whole world. Existing systems of religion can no longer guide humanity since they confine themselves to their own segments of society. We need a universal religion that can be equally applicable to all. In its light, we can strive toward equality, justice, and freedom together. Adhering to a universal religion, we can take care of all personal and social duties. In order to climb to the next step of human civilization, we must transcend petty religious disputes.

All religions of the world believe in the incarnation of God as messiah, prophet, or savior. Such a concept of God or godly manifestations restricts our worldview, and even forces us to divide humanity in the name of God. Identifying God as a personal being also prevents us from experiencing God in every human being. As a result, we do not respect our own brothers and sisters if they do not worship "our God." What ignorance to consider God to be merely our God and not the God of all! Unfortunately, that has been the case with many of the followers of God. The destiny of mankind lies in experiencing the God beyond "my God," "your God," or "their God."

Before becoming divine, we have to become fully evolved humans. Developing our humanity requires us to love and care for all. That is the condition for becoming a true human being. All the great ideals, positive attitudes, and creative forces grow in the heart after becoming a true human being, and we naturally move forward on the path of transformation. And, one day, the Divine unfolds within us.

All religions of the world have truth as their main goal. The goal is one, but the paths are many. By following any of those paths, one can attain the goal, but no one can attain peace from the path itself. Peace lies in the experience of truth. Out of ignorance, people have included hatred, jealousy, and discrimination based on race and color in religion. How can such attitudes be part of religion, and if they are, then how can such a religion be helpful for human growth? The dharma of mankind inspires all human beings to live with one another in peace and harmony. In order to adhere to that dharma, the universal religion, an individual or society has to be free of selfishness and narrow-mindedness. Once people can expand their worldview, establish a sense of equality, remove mutual differences, and search for the highest truth, they will find themselves to be more than just Hindus, Muslims, Christians, Jews, or Buddhists.

Selfishness is the root of all evil. As long as selfishness persists, there is no hope of having peace and happiness in life. Spiritual practices and efforts toward social harmony are in vain if we do not eliminate our selfishness. Selfishness is as bad for worldly people as it is for renunciates and monks. Love is the divine virtue all of us are trying to cultivate, and that virtue cannot coexist with selfishness. There are three innate qualities in all human beings: divine, human, and animal. Sensual slavery is an animal quality. Control of the senses and an inclination toward discipline are human qualities. Once the human qualities are awakened and a human being expresses them in his thoughts, speech, and actions, he naturally moves toward the Divine. If a human being focuses all his energy on sense pleasure and becomes self-centered, he falls into darkness. Such a person is just like an animal.

Another important factor for our growth and happiness is a proper understanding of others. In regard to any person, doctrine, or practice, before we come to a conclusion, we should free ourselves from any possible prejudice. No matter how good or reasonable a person's ideas are, we will not be able to grasp them if any prejudice exists in our minds. In order to grasp truth in its purity and integrity, the mind and intellect must be pure. That purity comes from having a burning desire to know the truth. An intellect preoccupied with attachment or aversion distrusts the content of any given theory. A polluted and skeptical intellect employs logic and reasoning to substantiate its own prejudices. One who hears the viewpoints of his opponents, and analyzes them impartially, is a genuine researcher. He is endowed with a pure intellect, and he is the one who studies constructively and arrives at the proper conclusion. That is the way to purify one's thoughts, which in turn purify one's speech and actions.

Without such purification, an individual cannot express his love to all equally. Purification is the most important prerequisite for undertaking any religious or spiritual discipline. Repetition of mantras, austerities, study of scriptures, and virtuous deeds are in vain if one's mind and intellect are not purified. Without inner purification, external cleanliness is of little value. Once a person has purified his inner life, the external life automatically follows. Since he is free from attachment, hatred, and jealousy, he remains above the conflicts and contradictions originating in the external world. Peace and harmony emanate from his being. He is happy within and becomes a channel to bring happiness to others.

Divine virtues grow in the fertile soil of love, compassion, generosity, and selflessness. These virtues are an inseparable part of all spiritual practices. Religion, morality, ethics, and social laws center around them. These qualities inspire us to open ourselves to divine communion. In fact, generosity, compassion, selflessness, and all other virtues are included in one experience—love. This is a rule: one receives love by loving others. One who practices nonviolence in one's thoughts, speech, and actions can follow the path of love.

In order to follow this path, we must surrender all our activities to the divine force. We must replace our egos with the presence of the Divine. From that infinite source, we can attain strength, conquer our weaknesses, and work toward the welfare of all. Without the guidance of the divine force within, all other forces remain disoriented.

Virtues help an aspirant find the company of the wise. From the wise, he learns the proper methods of contemplation and meditation. As he practices these teachings, the aspirant unfolds his inner potentials. At the final stage of his unfoldment, he realizes that this whole process from beginning to end has been inspired and guided by the divine force. This realization helps him surrender completely to the divine force, God. Once a person surrenders, his ego merges into the perfect "I-am-ness" of God. No distance remains between him and God. He sees the universe as a manifestation of God and stops searching for God in the outside world. He is in God and God is in him. The universe is part of him and he is part of the universe. Such a realized one loves all, considering them to be his own elaboration. Nonviolence in the form of love expresses itself spontaneously from his being. The senses and mind of the realized one do not have any desire to run from one object to another since he is established within. Anger, jealousy, and hatred disappear forever. He becomes an embodiment of inner strength. Such a person speaks as he thinks, and acts as he thinks and speaks. Free from fear, he practices nonviolence in his thoughts, speech, and actions. His way of life is exemplary.

In the world of today, one can be at peace with oneself only if one's neighbor is also at peace. The continents have come closer to each other. With the modern means of communication, this vast world of ours has contracted. We must learn to coexist and cultivate peace, harmony, love, and universal brotherhood. The whole world has to live like one family. The welfare of the entire world is every human being's concern. This is called humanism.

Chapter Seven

Culture and Civilization

THE ABILITY TO THINK systematically distinguishes human beings from the rest of creation. A natural setting, a good environment, and favorable circumstances inspire one to think and contemplate. The thinking process occurs both at individual and collective levels. Through the power of thought, humanity in the form of individuals and communities, continues to climb upward to the higher rungs of human evolution. The development of culture and civilization is entirely based on the gradual refinement of the thought process. At each stage, the level of thinking and contemplation attained becomes a foundation for the next level. New experiences are always guided by previous ones, and are, in fact, modified elaborations of previous experiences. This is a perennial process.

The culture, civilization, religion, and philosophy of any particular country or society are the result of the centuries of thought and contemplation of its people. With the passage of time, human beings assimilate experiences of success and failure. In an attempt to make their lives more fulfilling, they utilize the lessons derived from previous experience and refine their thinking process. This process goes on until one finds fulfillment in life. The refinement of the thinking process that helps make a person's life more comfortable and resourceful becomes the basis for improving his civilization and culture. Civilization and culture are not synonymous. Civilization encompasses values, religion, spirituality, the fine arts, and so on, whereas culture refers to the modes of external behavior, which may include the standard of living, fashion, etiquette, and a variety of other such aspects. Every country or society has its unique civilization and culture.

Being an old country, India has a very long history of culture and civilization. The philosophical and spiritual achievements of India are the outpourings of a stream of knowledge that sprang from the perennial truth and transcended the limitations of time and space. That profound heritage was derived from the great sages and thinkers who realized the truth directly and shared their wisdom with their fellow beings lovingly and selflessly as its patrons.

In Sanskrit, the language of ancient India, the words *samskriti* and *sabhyata* are used for civilization and culture. Etymologically, the word *samskriti* means "perfectly purified, refined, or processed." *Sabhyata* refers to "the quality of a cultured person." According to Panini, the eminent grammarian of the Sanskrit language, a cultured person is one who knows how to participate in the assembly of the elite. Every society has its own standards and in order to live in society properly, one must follow the rules and standards of that particular society. Social standards and recognized ways of interpersonal communication constitute the essence of culture. Samskriti or civilization, on the other hand, encompasses the more subtle virtues of human growth. Culture represents the nature of community life, especially that which corresponds to the external world, while civilization represents the inner life.

From generation to generation, humanity has experimented with new doctrines and ideals. One tries to live according to those ideals which will help one become more successful and creative. In the course of this ongoing process, human beings have realized that the perfection of both the inner and external life is of utmost importance. Without perfection within, and without organizing one's life in the external world, one cannot have peace of mind. By purifying and mastering inner life, one becomes civilized, and by organizing external life, one becomes cultured. The true growth of society depends on being fully civilized and cultured.

A human being is neither the body nor mind alone. Interfacing with one another, the body and mind receive their life force from the center of consciousness called Atman. It is the thread of the life force that connects the body with the mind; thus, the study of life includes a study of the body, mind and soul. In order to make a successful life, one must integrate worldly activities with spiritual life. One must find proper means and resources for maintaining one's physical existence. At the same time, one must find the peace of mind that flows from the center of consciousness.

What a human being thinks and inwardly experiences is expressed through his actions. The degree to which his thoughts, speech, and actions are integrated and balanced determines how evolved he is in his worldly and spiritual lives. Discriminating the real from the unreal is the first step on the path of realization. Without the discriminatory ability of our intellect, we cannot understand what perfection means. Without the power of discrimination, we can neither think properly nor resolve problems. Then, we fail to envision the real values of life. A civilized person or society is one that has attained the fullest expansion of discriminatory knowledge, has understood its rightful actions and obligations, and has the capacity to undertake those actions and meet those obligations. Envisioning high ideals and shaping one's life accordingly is the essence of civilization.

Civilization is the beauty of human life. The inner beauty of an individual or society expresses itself in the form of its worldview or perspective toward life itself. Once established, that particular worldview becomes the foundation for all its doctrines and principles. Until a given worldview, doctrine, or principle has become an inseparable part of civic awareness, it remains merely a theory under consideration. With the passage of time, when a philosophical thought becomes accepted by society and becomes the subliminal foundation of everyone's actions, then it becomes a part of the civilization of that given society. Civilization reflects truths which human beings recognize and assimilate in their prolonged search for felicity. The search for happiness never ends and so society continues to experiment with new ideas. Just as a child grows in its family environment, so does a society develop in its own environment. If a society continues on the path of purification, transformation, and spiritual upliftment, then there is hope for a long-lasting civilization. Contrary to that, if a society doesn't think of its long-term evolution and instead merely experiments with the external values of life, then its focus shifts toward culture, and values and experiences come and go in the form of fads. With fast-changing cultural values, customs, fashions, and external lifestyles, a society goes through a never-ending chain of dissatisfaction until it eventually seeks to reevaluate itself and reestablish itself on the foundation of civilization. Sooner or later, human beings feel the importance of building the structure of culture on the solid foundation of a valid civilization.

Peace and happiness are not found in worldly objects. For true happiness, we must purify our samskaras, the subtle impressions of our thoughts, speech, and actions, which influence every aspect of our lives. The purification of the subtle impressions of the past brighten our present and future. Our purification and improvement has an everlasting effect on us, as well as on society as a whole. The purification of individuals in the present contributes to the betterment of future generations. Civilization includes the contributions of the past and the present; it offers the gifts of its elders to the entire society. Civilization is an organized journey from imperfection to perfection, from failure to success.

According to the ancient thinkers, the Vedic heritage was not meant only for Indians; it was open to all of humanity. One can never find a passage in Vedic or Upanishadic literature saying "Let only Indians attain freedom, let only Indians have happiness, let only Indians have right thinking." Rather, in the Vedas and Upanishads one repeatedly reads "May all human beings cross all the hurdles in life, may all human beings attain only that which is good and auspicious. May all human beings acquire proper intellect so that they can discriminate right from wrong, good from bad, real from unreal, and may all human beings in all times and places be respected by one another." The codes of conduct described in the Upanishads are useful not for Indians alone, but for all who strive for the betterment of life.

No matter which culture, tradition, or nation we come from, for a happy and healthy life, we need to cultivate such virtues as forbearance, self-control, generosity, and compassion. These virtues are the hallmark of a spiritually based culture and civilization. Through these qualities, one attains success in the world as well as in spiritual life.

A society that emphasizes the study of the inner self, contemplation, and right conduct is an evolved society. Only such a society can have an evolved culture and civilization. Discrimination, dispassion, and constructive action are like the branches of the trees that grow from these seeds. The sages thus paid considerable attention to the purification of the samskaras, as well as to cleansing the body and polishing the intellectual faculty. Through the purification of previous impressions, one's whole life is purified. The means and methods for the purification of samskaras constitute civilization, whereas other objects which facilitate one's external life are part of culture. The means and methods for adjusting oneself and living comfortably in the external world belong to culture; how to enhance one's inner beauty and become the master of one's inner life are aspects of civilization.

Every human being has a culture, but that does not necessarily mean he or she is civilized. One may be an expert in dressing well but might fail to decorate one's inner life. A person clad in expensive clothes and ornaments might be wearing rags within. In our modern world, a person's status is measured by his standard of living, physical comforts, and luxuries, but the attainment of worldly means and resources are far from the sole factor for evaluating one's growth and true happiness. A person well-to-do in the external world may be afflicted with poverty in his spiritual life. There are people who live in fragile huts and have only the minimum necessities, but their lives are enriched with great virtues such as love, compassion, contentment, self-discipline, and right thinking. They are the ones who find joy in sharing another's pains, and sacrifice their comforts for the welfare of others. Thus, we can easily understand that culture is an ornament of the external aspects of our social life, whereas civilization is the blooming flower of spiritual living. Under the rejuvenating inspiration of the spiritual force, human beings keep moving toward the summum bonum of life, individually and collectively.

In ancient India, learned philosophers, thinkers, saints, and sages lived in solitude. Away from urban settings, they established their ashrams, spiritual and educational centers, in the lap of nature. The great thinkers of India lived in the forests at the cost of worldly comforts. They preferred to live a simple and peaceful life rather than collect objects for luxurious living. Indian philosophy was born not in the palaces but in the schools of nature where those great thinkers and philosophers lived. Those philosophers experimented with their doctrines and principles, and as a result illumined from inside, offered humanity revelations of the truth they experienced. Through practice, purification, and transformation, a philosopher turns into a sage. In this tradition a philosopher made his whole life a living laboratory. Such experimenters are the torchbearers of civilization. After realizing the truth within and validating his convictions through direct experience as well as logic, a sage defines his lifestyle so that his way of living and being can be exemplary to others. In ancient India, it was the lifestyle of the wise that set the standard of social life, not that of the kings, rich men, or warriors. The law-giver Manu, the writer of the ever-valid constitution of the human race, declared, "Having learned from the seers of this land, the people of the world should educate themselves and cultivate the right mode of living and being."

An advanced culture is that which is energetic, creative, and full of love and mutual understanding. The culture that does not encourage indulgence, vanity, hatred, jealousy, and selfishness, but replaces them with self-discipline, self-respect, love, friendship, and generosity is the culture most conducive to human growth. Such a culture can be expected only if human beings have envisioned a spiritually based civilization. A productive culture cannot stand without a living civilization, and vice versa. It is extremely difficult to sustain a highly evolved civilization without having a matching culture. Civilization is like a sword that needs to be sheathed in an appropriate scabbard. Without a sword, there is no use for a scabbard, and without the scabbard, the sword deteriorates.

Today, anyone venturing to teach and lead the human race must establish a balance between his doctrines and practical life. He must rise above his time-honored religious, cultural, and social conventions. He has to cultivate higher thoughts and look at the world and different communities as part of one family. Only then can he teach that which ought to be taught. Social reformation, cultural revolution, and an introduction to true civilization can be initiated after we have reformed and transformed ourselves individually.

Culture and civilization grow together, and influence and

enrich each other. The clothes we wear reflect our culture, but the inner life of the person who wears the clothes is structured in light of the civilization in which he is born and raised. A person's inner inclination is heavily influenced by a subtle force within. That force is the main factor in defining one's environment and background. It is the very core of civilization, and determines the direction of culture. However, once that culture is achieved it then reflects back on the civilization. Thus, civilization is the source of inspiration, whereas culture evolves in order to meet the demands of that inspiration. If polished properly, culture can serve the prime motive of civilization; if neglected, it can damage its own foundation. Being invisible and abstract, the principles of civilization cannot be comprehended easily, whereas being visible and outward-oriented, the culture of a particular group within the human race can be measured. In a short period of time cultural values can be adopted and experimented with, and the results experienced. However, the impact of civilization is long-lasting.

Civilization requires several centuries to reach maturity. By following a particular lifestyle and practicing a particular philosophy, the people of a given society imbue their lives with its philosophy. When those ideals and philosophical disciplines enter the unconscious, it is called civilization, firm and stable. We use and enjoy the things that correspond to culture, but we live with the principles and ideals that correspond to the domain of civilization. We may accept or disregard the cultural values of our lifetime, but it takes several lifetimes to absorb the principles of civilization. It is almost impossible to disregard them once they are absorbed. At a very subtle level, a given civilization goes through gradual change as people from various cultures and civilizations interact with each other. Interactions between cultures create samskaras in people's minds, individually and collectively. A significant change, however, can be observed after centuries of exchange.

A civilization which is not open to interaction with other groups of people cannot maintain its excellence for very long. If people from a particular culture think that they are superior and do not welcome ideas from outside, they damage their culture and civilization seriously. Openness to new ideas and an ability to absorb them are the main factors for the sustenance and growth of a civilization. A pond whose source has become blocked and yet continues to drain will eventually dry up. Similarly, a civilization that shuts itself off from other civilizations becomes stagnant and deteriorates, and as a result loses its capacity to meet the ever-changing challenges of its contemporary society.

We should not forget the true meaning of freedom. In the context of culture and civilization, the concept of freedom must not be confined to material, political, or economic factors alone. True freedom means freedom of thought. Through this freedom, we can attain philosophical and spiritual wealth. Broad-mindedness, a sense of equality, and the realization that this whole world is one family are the results of independent thinking. Independent thinking means freedom from all prejudices, superficial beliefs, and superstitious practices. Spirituality, if revived and properly restored, can save the whole world from the destructive blows of materialism. We must make up our minds to reestablish the higher values of civilization and to start practicing that philosophy which is essential for growth here and hereafter.

GLOSSARY

Antahkarana The inner instrument. The intellect (buddhi), ego (ahamkara), sensory-motor mind (manas), and storehouse of memories (chitta) are considered to be the inner instruments of cognition.

Arjuna The protagonist of the Bhagavad Gita, who chose Sri Krishna as his charioteer in the war against the Kauravas. Arjuna represents the individual self or the student, and Krishna is the universal self or teacher. Arjuna means "one who makes sincere efforts." Historically, Arjuna belongs to the famous royal clan Bharata, after which the subcontinent India (called Bharata in Hindi) is named.

Atman The pure self. According to Indian philosophy, the pure self is eternal; its essential nature is existence, consciousness, and bliss. It permeates the waking, dreaming, and deep sleep states and remains above all mundane pains and pleasures.

Brahman The absolute reality, pure consciousness. According to Advaita Vedanta philosophy, Brahman is the absolute nondual reality, and its essential nature is existence, consciousness, and bliss. There is a perfect identity between the pure self and Brahman; the difference or duality between Brahman and the pure self is mere illusion.

Chitta The storehouse of memory, the unconscious mind.

Dharma The eternal law that holds and maintains the individual as well as social life. In the Eastern tradition, it signifies philosophy, spirituality, and discipline, which if practiced could guide humanity toward its highest destiny. It also refers to one's duty or destiny in life.

Ida   One of the three nadis, corresponding to lunar energy and situated on the left side of the spinal column.

Karma   Action. It includes the law of actions and reactions, the driving forces of one's present and future.

Karma Yoga   The "discipline of action" in which selfless action without desire for personal gain is cultivated. In this way one gradually cuts back on the number of new impressions (the seeds of future action and of rebirth) gathered by the subconscious. One's actions are gradually purified as meditation is slowly brought into active life.

Mantra   A set of syllables, sounds, or words, received from the teacher during initiation for meditation and spiritual advancement.

Nadi   An energy channel. According to the yogic tradition, there are 72,000 nadis, of which 14 are the important ones. Out of these, ida, pingala, and sushumna are the most important nadis, especially for spiritual purposes.

Nyaya   One of the classical Indian philosophical systems, devoting its attention primarily to the science of logic.

Pingala   One of the three major energy channels situated along the right side of the spinal column, corresponding to the solar energy in the body.

Prajapati   The lord of all subjects; a term for the creator of the universe.

Prana   One of the major vital forces. It is marked by inhalation or the taking in of fresh life essence. The heart, lungs, and brain are considered to be the main seats of the vital force.

Pranayama   The science of gradually lengthening and controlling the physical breath in order to gain control over the movements of prana through the subtle body in higher stages of the practice. It is the fourth of the eight steps of yoga described by Patanjali.

Sabhyata Lifestyle and standard of living of a civilized person; culture and civilization of a particular community indicative of its unique characteristics.

Sadhana Literally, "accomplishing" or "fulfilling." Sadhana is the word for a student's sincere efforts along a particular path of practice toward self-realization.

Samadhi Spiritual absorption; the eighth rung of raja yoga. The tranquil state of mind in which fluctuations of the mind no longer arise.

Samskriti The quality of being cultured or refined.

Shakti The power. The dynamic aspect of consciousness, the source of the manifest world and its activities.

Shraddha Faith. Faith is a divine quality and an essential aspect of one's spiritual practice. Such faith does not rely on the knowledge of the scriptures; rather it comes through spontaneous experience from within.

Sushumna The central nadi through which the dormant force of kundalini arises and unites with supreme consciousness, Shiva, in sahasrara, the crown center.

Upanishads The later part of the Vedas are called the Upanishads. The Upanishads are those profound spiritual scriptures which are studied under the guidance of an enlightened preceptor.

Vairagya Dispassion or nonattachment. According to the Bhagavad Gita, one does not necessarily need to renounce the world or what one needs, but one should perform his duties lovingly, skillfully, and selflessly, remaining unattached to the fruits of his actions.

Vedanta The system of Indian philosophy that expounds the theory of nondualism.

Vedas   The treasury of knowledge. Vedas are the most ancient scriptures of the world.

Yoga   The system of Indian philosophy systematized and codified by the sage Patanjali. It also refers to the practical aspect of any philosophy, particularly Sankhya. Literally it means "yoke," referring to the uniting of the individual self and the universal self.

About the Author

BORN IN 1925 in northern India, Swami Rama was raised from early childhood by a great yogi and saint of Bengal who lived in the foothills of the Himalayas. In his youth he practiced the various disciplines of yoga science and philosophy in the traditional monasteries of the Himalayas and studied closely with many spiritual adepts, including Mahatma Gandhi, Sri Aurobindo, and Rabindranath Tagore. He also traveled to Tibet to study with his grandmaster.

He received his higher education at Bangalore, Prayaga, Varanasi, and Oxford University, England. At the age of twenty-four he became Shankaracharya of Karvirpitham in South India, the highest spiritual position in India. During this term he had a tremendous impact on the spiritual customs of that time: he dispensed with useless formalities and rituals, made it possible for all segments of society to worship in the temples, and encouraged the instruction of women in meditation. He renounced the dignity and prestige of this high office in 1952 to return to the Himalayas to intensify his meditative practices.

After completing an intense meditative practice in the cave monasteries, he emerged with the determination to serve humanity, particularly to bring the teachings of the East to the West. With the encouragement of his master, Swami Rama began his task by studying Western philosophy and psychology, and teaching Eastern philosophy at Western universities. He worked as a medical consultant in London and assisted in parapsychological research in Moscow. He then returned to India, where he established an ashram in Rishikesh. He completed his degree in homeopathy at the medical college in Darbhanga in 1960. He came to the United States in 1969, bringing his knowledge and wisdom to the West. His teachings combine Eastern spirituality with modern Western therapies.

Swami Rama was a freethinker, guided by his direct experience and inner wisdom, and he encouraged his students to be guided in the same way. He often told them, "I am a messenger, delivering the wisdom of the Himalayan sages of my tradition. My job is to introduce you to the teacher within."

Swami Rama came to America upon the invitation of Dr. Elmer Green of the Menninger Foundation of Topeka, Kansas, as a consultant in a research project investigating the voluntary control of involuntary states. He participated in experiments that helped to revolutionize scientific thinking about the relationship between body and mind, amazing scientists by his demonstrating, under laboratory conditions, precise conscious control of autonomic physical responses and mental functioning, feats previously thought to be impossible.

Swami Rama founded the Himalayan International Institute of Yoga Science and Philosophy, the Himalayan Institute Hospital Trust in India, and many centers thoughout the world. He is the author of numerous books on health, meditation, and the yogic scriptures. Swami Rama left his body in November 1996.

The main building of the national headquarters, Honesdale, Pa.

THE HIMALAYAN INSTITUTE

FOUNDED IN 1971 by Swami Rama, the Himalayan Institute has been dedicated to helping people grow physically, mentally, and spiritually by combining the best knowledge of both the East and the West. Institute programs emphasize holistic health, yoga, and meditation, but the Institute is much more than its programs.

Our national headquarters is located on a beautiful 400-acre campus in the rolling hills of the Pocono Mountains of northeastern Pennsylvania. The atmosphere here is one to foster growth, increased inner awareness, and calm. Our grounds provide a wonderfully peaceful and healthy setting for our seminars and extended programs. Students from around the world join us here to attend programs in such diverse areas as hatha yoga, meditation, stress reduction, Ayurveda, nutrition, Eastern philosophy, psychology, and other subjects. Whether the programs are for weekend meditation retreats, week-long seminars on spirituality, months-long residential programs, or holistic health services, the attempt here is to provide an environment of gentle inner progress. We invite you to join with us in the ongoing process of personal growth and development.

The Institute is a nonprofit organization. Your membership in the Institute helps to support its programs. Please call or write for information on becoming a member.

Institute Programs, Services, and Facilities

All Institute programs share an emphasis on conscious, holistic living and personal self-development. You may enjoy any of a number of diverse programs, including:

Special weekend or extended seminars to teach skills and techniques for increasing your ability to be healthy and enjoy life

Meditation retreats and advanced meditation instruction

Vegetarian cooking and nutritional training

Hatha yoga and exercise workshops

Residential programs for self-development

The Institute's Center for Health and Healing offers holistic health services and Ayurvedic Rejuvenation Programs.

The Institute publishes a free *Quarterly Guide to Programs and Other Offerings*. To request a copy, or for further information, call 800-822-4547, fax 717-253-9078, e-mail himalaya@epix.net, or write the Himalayan Institute/RR 1, Box 400/Honesdale, PA 18431.

The main building of the hospital, outside Dehra Dun

Himalayan Institute Hospital and Medical City

A major aspect of the Institute's work around the world is its support of a comprehensive Medical City in the Garhwal region of the foothills of the Himalayas. A bold vision to bring medical services to 15 million mostly poor people who have little or no health care in northern India began modestly in 1989 with an outpatient program in Uttar Pradesh.

Today that vision has grown to include a fully operational, 500-bed, state-of-the-art hospital between Dehra Dun and Rishikesh; a Medical College and nursing school, a combined therapy program that joins the best of modern, Western medicine and the time-tested wisdom of traditional methods of health care; a rural development program that has adopted more than 150 villages; and housing facilities for staff, students and patients' relatives.

The project was conceived, designed and led by Swami Rama, who was a native of this part of India. He always envisioned joining the best knowledge of the East and West. And that is what is occurring at this medical facility, 125 miles north of New Delhi.

Guided by the Himalayan Institute Hospital Trust, the umbrella body for the entire project, the hospital, medical city and rural development program are considered models of health care for the whole of India and for medically under-served people worldwide.

Construction, expansion, and the fund-raising necessary to accomplish it all continues. The hospital is now one of the best-equipped hospitals in India, but more can always be done.

We welcome financial support to help with this and other projects. If you would like further information, please call our national headquarters in Honesdale, PA at 800-822-4547.

The Himalayan Institute Press

The Himalayan Institute Press has long been regarded as "The Resource for Holistic Living." We publish dozens of titles, as well as audio and video tapes, that offer practical methods for harmonious living and inner balance. Our approach addresses the whole person—body, mind, and spirit—integrating the latest scientific knowledge with ancient healing and self-development techniques.

As such, we offer a wide array of titles on physical and psychological health and well-being, spiritual growth through meditation and other yogic practices, and the means to stay inspired through reading sacred scriptures and ancient philosophical teachings.

Our health sidelines include The Neti Pot, the ideal tool for sinus and allergy sufferers, and The Breath Pillow, a unique tool for learning health-supportive breathing—the diaphragmatic breath.

Subscriptions are available to a bimonthly magazine, *Yoga International*, which offers thought-provoking articles on all aspects of meditation and yoga, including yoga's sister science, Ayurveda.

Call 800-822-4547, fax 717-251-7812, or e-mail hibooks@epix.net for a free catalog.